COMMUNITY
CONNECTIONS
AND YOUR PLC AT WORK®

A GUIDE TO ENGAGING FAMILIES

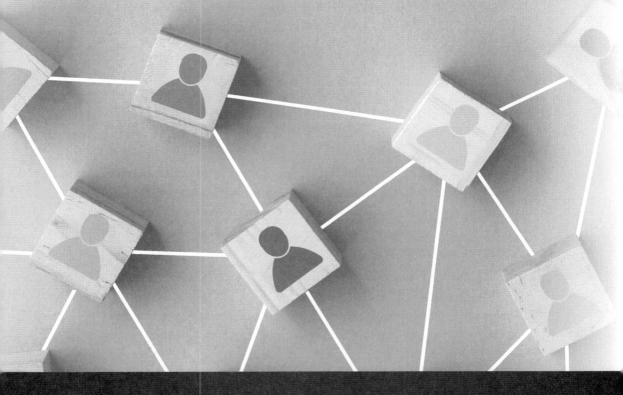

NATHANIEL PROVENCIO

Solution Tree | Press

a division of
Solution Tree

555 North Morton Street
Bloomington, IN 47404
800.733.6786 (toll free) / 812.336.7700
FAX: 812.336.7790

email: info@SolutionTree.com
SolutionTree.com

Visit **go.SolutionTree.com/PLCbooks** to download the free reproducibles in this book.

Printed in the United States of America

Library of Congress Cataloging-in-Publication Data

Names: Provencio, Nathaniel, author.
Title: Community connections and your PLC at work : a guide to engaging families / Nathaniel Provencio.
Description: Bloomington, IN : Solution Tree Press, 2021. | Includes bibliographical references and index.
Identifiers: LCCN 2020020330 (print) | LCCN 2020020331 (ebook) | ISBN 9781951075194 (paperback) | ISBN 9781951075200 (ebook)
Subjects: LCSH: Professional learning communities--United States. | Education--Parent participation--United States. | School improvement programs--United States.
Classification: LCC LB1731 .P739 2021 (print) | LCC LB1731 (ebook) | DDC 371.2/070973--dc23
LC record available at https://lccn.loc.gov/2020020330
LC ebook record available at https://lccn.loc.gov/2020020331

Solution Tree
Jeffrey C. Jones, CEO
Edmund M. Ackerman, President

Solution Tree Press
President and Publisher: Douglas M. Rife
Associate Publisher: Sarah Payne-Mills
Art Director: Rian Anderson
Managing Production Editor: Kendra Slayton
Senior Production Editor: Suzanne Kraszewski
Senior Editor: Amy Rubenstein
Copy Editor: Evie Madsen
Proofreader: Elisabeth Abrams
Text and Cover Designer: Laura Cox
Editorial Assistants: Sarah Ludwig and Elijah Oates

For Evan and Lily

ACKNOWLEDGMENTS

Solution Tree Press would like to thank the following reviewers:

Rachel Garrett
Principal
LISD STEM Academy at
    Valley Ridge Elementary
Lewisville, Texas

Deanna Herrera
Assistant Principal
Bosque Farms Elementary
Bosque Farms, New Mexico

Wes Kanawyer
Principal
Woodgate Intermediate School
Waco, Texas

Carlos Lawrence
Assistant Principal
Glastonbury-East Hartford
Magnet School
Glastonbury, Connecticut

Jennifer Mattingly
Principal
McAuliffe Elementary
Highland Village, Texas

Luke Spielman
Principal
Park View Middle School
Mukwonago, Wisconsin

Vanessa Stuart
Principal
Degan Elementary School
Lewisville, Texas

Visit **go.SolutionTree.com/PLCbooks** to download the free reproducibles in this book.

TABLE OF CONTENTS

Reproducible pages are in italics.

ABOUT THE AUTHOR

 **Nathaniel Provencio, MEd,** is an associate superintendent in Prince William County, Virginia. Under his leadership as principal, Minnieville Elementary School, a Title I school with a culturally and linguistically diverse student population, was recognized as a model professional learning community (PLC) and was the 2019 winner of the prestigious DuFour Award (Solution Tree, n.d.). In addition, Nathaniel led Minnieville Elementary's efforts to become a Virginia Distinguished Title I School.

In recognition of his ongoing work to enhance effective classroom instruction, promote collaboration among all stakeholders, and grow family and community engagement, he was honored as the 2017 Prince William County Principal of the Year, 2017 *Washington Post* Principal of the Year, and 2019 Virginia Principal of the Year.

In addition to leading Minnieville Elementary, Nathaniel is an award-winning leader in advocating for local community involvement and business engagement in economically and culturally diverse schools. He is a sought-after presenter and has presented at regional, state, and national conferences in the areas of PLCs, family engagement, and effective literacy frameworks.

Nathaniel earned a bachelor's degree in education from the University of North Alabama and a master's degree in education administration from George Mason University. In 2018, he was recognized as an Alumni Exemplar by George Mason University.

To learn more about Nathaniel Provencio's work, visit @ProvenPrincipal on Twitter.

To book Nathaniel Provencio for professional development, contact pd@SolutionTree.com.

CONNECTING YOUR PLC COMMUNITY

M ost of us have heard the widely used African proverb, "It takes a village to raise a child." This saying articulates the importance of having a network of adults working together to raise and educate a nation's children. It connotes a sense of self-sacrifice and communal partnership in taking care of the most precious resource we have as human beings—our children. Since the beginning of time, communities around the world have created frameworks for caring for and educating children. Doing so provides children with a high level of protection and safety and allows the culture of the community to educate and shape them.

This proverb implies collaboration. Can you imagine a school in which every educator, parent, and community member actively collaborates for the well-being of each student? This sense of community is what this book is all about. It is about utilizing the effective elements and practices of the Professional Learning Communities at Work® (PLC at Work®) process as PLC at Work architects Richard DuFour, Robert Eaker, and Rebecca DuFour (DuFour, DuFour, Eaker, Many, & Mattos, 2016) outline to enhance a school's efforts to raise parent, family, and community involvement and engagement. The purpose of every PLC is to ensure *all* students learn at high levels. For this to truly happen, *all* adults invested in the success of our children must be a collaborative part of the PLC process.

It is virtually impossible for a school to have high test scores and high levels of student achievement without having a strong collaborative culture with involved and engaged parents, families, and community members. However, for many schools— especially economically disadvantaged and culturally diverse schools struggling with student achievement—fostering high levels of parent, family, and community involvement and engagement can often be a challenge. This was the case for the school I began leading as a new principal. This book will examine how the staff's focus on implementing the PLC process and on family involvement and engagement helped turn around the school and led it to become a model PLC and the winner of the 2019 DuFour Award (Solution Tree, n.d.).

In the spring of 2010, I had the privilege and honor of being selected to serve as the principal of Minnieville Elementary School in Prince William County, Virginia. Prior to this appointment, I served as a third-grade teacher for six amazing years and as an assistant principal in two different elementary schools for three years. At the time of my appointment, I felt I had a wealth of instructional and leadership experiences to prepare me for my new position. I quickly found out, however, that I was in over my head with the overwhelming tasks before me as the new principal of Minnieville Elementary.

Minnieville Elementary is in the heart of Dale City, a neighborhood in the city of Woodbridge, Virginia. Built in 1972, this established school has a rich history. In the early 1970s and 1980s, Minnieville Elementary was a predominately White, middle-class school. Most students had parents who commuted to Washington, DC, to work in various professional, government, and military occupations. Yet, as in most neighborhoods, demographics evolved over time. By the year 2000, Minnieville Elementary had become one of the most culturally and economically diverse schools in the United States (see table I.1). Students enrolled at Minnieville Elementary now represent countries from all over the world. The largest student populations represent Central and South American countries such as El Salvador, Honduras, Guatemala, Peru, and Bolivia. The school also has many students from West African countries such as Ghana, the Ivory Coast, Sierra Leone, and Nigeria. Additionally, it has a rising Middle Eastern student population representing countries including Iraq, Afghanistan, Pakistan, and Syria (Prince William County Public Schools, 2018). The relatively rapid growth of the area and changing cultural and economic conditions had a huge impact on the academic growth of the school.

Most Minnieville Elementary students are *second-language learners* (see table I.2), meaning English is not their first language. In addition to the cultural diversity of the school, over 75 percent of students are economically disadvantaged. A large percentage of the school's families is immigrants, and although working to contribute to the betterment of themselves and their families, they often live in a state of uncertainty and fear of changing immigration laws and economic insecurity.

Table I.1: Minnieville Elementary Student Demographics, 2017–2018

Race	Percent
Hispanic of any race	50.7
American Indian or Alaskan	0.2
Asian	9.5
Black/African American	27.5
Hawaiian or Pacific Islander	0.2
White	8.7
Two or more races	3.3

Source: Adapted from Prince William County Public Schools, 2018.

Table I.2: Students Participating in Special Services as of June 2018

Program	Number	Percent
Economically disadvantaged	397	76.8
English learners	277	53.6
Special education	55	10.6
Title I	517	100

Source: Adapted from Prince William County Public Schools, 2018.

All these social, cultural, and economic factors impact the academic success of Minnieville Elementary students. When I became principal, Minnieville Elementary was ranked in the bottom 25th percentile on end-of-year state assessments (SchoolDigger, n.d.).

During my first year at Minnieville Elementary, the assistant principal and I spent time throughout each day talking to teachers about the school's culture, students' instructional needs, school- and community-related problems, and so on. When asked about the needs of the school, teachers would usually articulate the need for more collaboration, structure, support, and administrative guidance. There was very little sense of urgency for them to address the fact that their school was performing in the bottom quartile of all schools in the state. It was almost as though the entire staff had settled on mediocrity and, because of its challenging demographics, there was a feeling that nothing really could be done. An apathetic teacher culture had created an apathetic parent culture, and perhaps vice versa. It's a very sobering feeling to be a turnaround school principal tasked with having to *rebuild a culture from the ground up*; this means reinvigorating the school's soul and implementing strong frameworks, processes, and systems to revitalize the school community.

I was introduced to the PLC process as an assistant principal; I knew the tenets of the process would provide the structure for growth Minnieville Elementary needed. I knew if my entire staff could carefully align its efforts with the three big ideas of PLCs (a focus on learning, a focus on collaboration, and a focus on results [DuFour et al., 2016]), the school could begin to experience success. I also knew that a strong PLC culture has a collaboratively developed vision and mission, which the staff uses to maintain a laser-like focus on learning for all.

Teams in a PLC use four critical questions as vital tools to structure and enhance their collaboration and engage in a cycle of continuous improvement (DuFour et al., 2016).

1. What do we want our students to learn?

2. How will we know when students have learned it?

3. How will we respond when students haven't learned it?

4. How will we extend and enrich the learning for students who have learned it?

I thought if my staff could keep their focus on these attributes—the big ideas and the four critical questions of a PLC—then the school would begin to see incremental growth in student achievement, year after year. Since implementing the PLC process in 2010, Minnieville Elementary became a Prince William County School of Excellence, a 2016 Virginia Distinguished Title I School, and, in 2019, the winner of the prestigious DuFour Award.

Although as a school, we are tremendously proud of our efforts to improve student academic achievement using the PLC process, this book is actually about how staff utilize the PLC process beyond the walls of the school building. The goal of this book is to give administrators and other leaders in an established PLC school culture a road map for enhancing parent, family, and community involvement and engagement utilizing foundational elements of PLCs.

As staff moved from the initiating stage to the sustaining stage in its PLC development, parent, family, and community involvement and engagement grew as well. This growth was not by chance! Minnieville Elementary leaders and all staff systematically focus on this area. The research fully supports the fact that the more parents, family, and community members connect and invest in their neighborhood school, the higher the school will perform. Parent involvement in education is crucial (Chen, 2020; National Coalition for Parent Involvement in Education, 2006). No matter their income or background, students with involved parents are more likely to have higher grades and test scores, attend school regularly, have better social skills, show improved behavior, and adapt well to school. This book outlines how Minnieville

Elementary is disrupting this narrative and growing its parent, family, and community involvement and engagement.

In This Book

This book takes research-based elements of the PLC process and overlays them with a strategic plan to enhance a school's parent, family, and community engagement. It is not intended to cover every aspect of the PLC process; rather, it highlights those elements and structures of a PLC that the staff and I utilized at Minnieville Elementary to expand our PLC to frame and improve interactions with parents, families, and community members to further support the mission of learning for all.

Chapter 1 provides a brief overview of the PLC process and how elements relate to parent, family, and community involvement. Chapter 1 also explores mission and vision, and how to create ownership and buy-in among parents, families, and community members. Chapter 2 introduces the concept of a family-engagement guiding coalition. Chapter 3 examines how to include a family focus in the school mission and vision. Chapter 4 looks at the importance of having a customer-centric culture in your PLC. Chapter 5 discusses creating a focus on learning with families. Chapter 6 applies the PLC big idea of collaboration to a school's work with parents and families. Chapter 7 looks at how to keep the focus on results for parents and families. The appendix features activities and strategies to help guide your work.

Throughout this book, you will find several repeating features. Each chapter contains Parent Voices, which are views from parents of Minnieville Elementary students who have experienced firsthand how the PLC process can transform the relationship between a school and families. There are also Administrator Voices and Community Partner Voices throughout. Each chapter concludes with Next Steps and reproducible forms with questions school leaders and staff can consider when implementing these processes in their own schools.

Final Thoughts

An African proverb states, "A family is like a forest. When you are outside, it is dense. When you are inside, you see that each tree has its place." In a PLC culture, every student, teacher, staff member, parent, and family and community member has a place and is vital to the operation of the school. Schools and districts that are well versed and knowledgeable on the PLC process will find that integrating elements of the process to enhance family engagement in schools may be as seamless as any effort to raise results in any content area. Schools and districts that are new to the PLC process and are interested in seeking out practical and tangible steps in addressing family engagement will still find this book exceptionally helpful. My goal for this book is to serve as both an inspiration and guide for school staff, school leaders, teachers, and district leaders implementing the PLC process and working to enhance parent, family, and community involvement and engagement.

CHAPTER 1

SETTING THE STAGE

*Let us put our minds together and see what
life we can make for our children.*

—Sitting Bull

n 2011 I had the opportunity to take a team of school-based leaders to Richmond, Virginia, to attend an all-day conference on PLCs. As a school, we were in the early initiating stage in our PLC development; this workshop was a chance to bring our school leaders up to speed on the most current practices related to the PLC process. I remember sitting in the audience, mesmerized by the knowledge and insights of Richard and Rebecca DuFour, architects of the PLC at Work process. Their pragmatic, common-sense approach, stories, lessons, and sense of urgency to utilize the PLC process were overwhelmingly inspiring for our team. By the end of the day, it was clear to our team that the PLC process would become our framework for excellence as a school, and in the years since, PLC has become the lens through which Minnieville leaders and staff members examine every potential action.

Many schools claim to be PLCs; in reality, however, they might just be what PLC at Work experts Richard DuFour, Rebecca DuFour, Robert Eaker, Thomas W. Many, and Mike Mattos (2016) call *PLC lite*—implementing some elements of the process at a surface level, but never addressing the deep transformation schools must undergo to become PLCs. In fact, schools operating in the sustaining stage of the PLC process often say they will never truly arrive because they are on a journey of continuous improvement. There is always more improvement to be done!

PLCs are more than having a catchy mission, holding structured meetings, and occasionally talking about data; PLCs are about sustaining a culture of improvement.

As DuFour and colleagues (2016) explain in *Learning by Doing: A Handbook for Professional Learning Communities at Work*, a PLC is "an ongoing process in which educators work collaboratively in recurring cycles of collective inquiry and action research to achieve better results for the students they serve" (p. 10). In the definition, *educators* are the adults in a school—leaders, teachers, staff members, and so on.

In this definition, *recurring cycles of collective inquiry and action research* means to actively work in a pattern of continuous improvement. So, teachers and collaborative teams are feverishly working to find ways a student can improve his or her academic success and meet learning goals. In teams, teachers talk through ideas, share strategies, and look at data to seek a root cause of either why a student isn't meeting the standard or how a student can work to exceed the standard. Finally, the term *results* is key in this definition of a PLC. The efforts of a PLC are not about the intentions of the adults, but about the results they achieve.

At Minnieville Elementary, success in improving student achievement using the PLC process led the staff and I to undertake a bold re-examination of this definition and apply it to parents, families, and community members. What if parents, families, and community members are *educators*? We know students' first educators are their parents and family members. Regardless of a family's economic situation or cultural background, all families have a wealth of knowledge that schools can tap into and utilize when developing relationships and partnerships. Some parents and family members actively volunteer and share their input with teachers. However, teachers must ask others to provide input and suggestions about their children's education. Still others may never set foot on school grounds. Regardless of how involved parents and family members are at the school level, at the end of the day, the student will still go home to his or her family and learn the lessons they teach, whether academic, cultural, social, or emotional. Parents and family members model for children what to do or not to do. All adults in the child's life are educators—for better or worse.

An early step in the PLC process for parent and family involvement is to define exactly what the school wants to accomplish. What are parent and family involvement and engagement? This chapter then examines mission and vision, values and goals, the three big ideas of a PLC, and the four critical questions.

Involvement *Versus* Engagement

Author and educator Larry Ferlazzo (2011) states the following about parent and family involvement versus engagement:

> A school striving for family involvement often leads with its mouth—identifying projects, needs, and goals and then telling parents how they can contribute. A school striving for parent engagement, on the other

hand, tends to lead with its ears—listening to what parents think, dream, and worry about.

It's not that family involvement is bad. Almost all the research says that any kind of increased parent interest and support of students can help. But almost all the research also says that family engagement can produce even better results—for students, for families, for schools, and for their communities (Ferlazzo & Hammond, 2009, p. 12).

At Minnieville Elementary, the staff and I decided we wanted parents and families to be both involved and engaged; we wanted parents and families to understand how they can contribute and have opportunities to do so, but ultimately, we want them to be partners engaged in striving for the school's mission and achieving its vision.

Mission and Vision

When schools are implementing the PLC process to transform school culture, one of the first things staff must do is develop a clear mission and vision. In a PLC, the *mission* statement answers the question, Why do we exist? (DuFour et al., 2016). The mission of a PLC, or its fundamental purpose, is to ensure high levels of learning for all. A PLC's mission statement will align with this purpose.

A school's *vision* addresses the question, What do we hope to become? (DuFour et al., 2016). It is the ideal a staff are trying to live up to; it provides "direction and a basis for assessing both the current reality of the school and potential strategies, programs, and procedures to improve that reality" (Mattos, DuFour, DuFour, Eaker, & Many, 2016, p. 22). At Minnieville Elementary, our mission states that each member of our community will "Soar for Excellence." Our vision states that we will do that by focusing on a *commitment* to best PLC practices, *collaboration* in everything we do, and a strong focus on our *community*. Schools across the United States have worked to develop exemplary mission and vision statements and actively utilize them to give their schools and districts clear direction and purpose on why they exist and what they must become in order to ensure all students are learning at high levels. Consider the following examples.

- Battlefield Primary School's (Catoosa County, Georgia) mission is "Everyone, Everyday," and the vision is "Collaborate, Understand Data, Be Committed to Student Learning" (www.catoosa.k12.ga.us).

- Southside Elementary's (Shelbyville, Kentucky) mission is "Smart, Strong, and Selfless," and the vision is "Inspired Learning, Living, and Leading" (www.shelby.kyschools.us/Southside).

- Casa Grande Union High School District's (Casa Grande, Arizona) mission is "To inspire excellence by providing globally competitive educational and career opportunities for all students," and the vision is "All Living the Pursuit of Excellence for Lifetime Achievement" (www.cguhsd.org).

- Hardin County Middle School's (Savannah, Tennessee) mission is "To engage, equip, and empower our students with the skills and attitudes vital to succeed as community and global citizens," and the vision is "Learn, Lead, Serve" (https://hardincoschools.com).

Just like major corporations have a clear mission and vision that sets the tone and articulates the culture of the organization, schools should as well. Think about your school culture and the community it serves. As a PLC, your staff should be able to articulate the mission and vision. Can parents, families, and community members articulate your school's mission and vision? If not, why not? A school's vision and mission are not simply for teachers and staff; they are for every member of the school community. At Minnieville Elementary, we did everything we could to promote, communicate, and make sure our parents and families were on board with the school's mission and vision.

Values and Goals

In addition to developing a vision and mission, Minnieville staff also adhered to collective commitments. Collective commitments answer the question, How must we behave to achieve our vision? (DuFour et al., 2016). Minnieville collective commitments state:

> As a professional teacher at Minnieville Elementary, I understand that I will be an active, positive, and contributing member of my school and grade-level professional learning community. I understand that I will utilize my strengths and talents to focus on effective instruction, collaboration, and student learning results. I understand that I will collaboratively construct and adhere to my team's norms and grade-level goals. I understand that I will continue to grow as a professional learner in an effort to improve my professional practice and the expertise of my team. I will ensure that my actions will promote the academic and social growth of each student and family at Minnieville Elementary.

Goals are the targets and timelines that answer the question, How will we mark our progress? (DuFour et al., 2016). They help staff establish their priorities.

At Minnieville, we also examined the three big ideas of a PLC and the four critical questions to consider how to apply these PLC foundational concepts to parent and family engagement and involvement.

The Three Big Ideas

In a PLC, there are three big ideas that drive the work of the school. According to DuFour et al. (2016), those big ideas are as follows.

1. A focus on learning

2. A collaborative culture and collective responsibility

3. A results orientation

A Focus on Learning

As mentioned previously, "the fundamental purpose of the school is to ensure all students learn at high levels" (DuFour et al., 2016, p. 11). PLCs focus on *both* student and adult learning. Obviously, student learning is essential because that is a school's primary function. Without teacher learning, however, student learning won't happen. In a PLC, teachers are lifelong learners engaged in ongoing efforts to learn from one another, enhancing their pedagogical practices at every opportunity.

In the quest to improve parent and family involvement and engagement at Minnieville Elementary, my staff and I thought parent and family learning should also be a focus for the school. School staff should seek ways to enhance parents' knowledge of school structures, standards, and best practices for home and school. All interactions with parents and families should have this focus, so parents and families are more informed about their children's learning and how they can become better support people and advocates than they were when they first walked into the school building.

A Collaborative Culture and Collective Responsibility

In a PLC, "educators must work collaboratively and take collective responsibility for the success of each student" (DuFour et al., 2016, p. 11). Collaboration is not optional. Thus, members of PLCs "work *interdependently* to achieve *common goals* for which members are *mutually accountable*" (DuFour et al., 2016, p. 12). Collaboration increases buy-in and empowerment. At Minnieville Elementary, when considering how to increase parent and family involvement and engagement, the staff and I knew we had to include parents and families in our collaborative efforts. After all, parents and families are important stakeholders in their children's education, and they share common goals with the school. We decided to include multiple stakeholders in our decision making—not simply administrators, teachers, and staff, but also parents and families. *A culture and focus on collaboration* mean that no decision and action in a school will ever be made by one person in isolation.

A Results Orientation

Finally, a school operating as a PLC focuses on *results*—or evidence of student learning (DuFour et al., 2016). Results are far different from intentions. Staff in a PLC use results to "inform and improve their professional practice and respond to individual students who need intervention and enrichment" (DuFour et al., 2016, p. 12). As a PLC, your school is transparent with sharing data and results with collaborative teacher teams. It seems only natural to extend this results orientation to interactions with parents and families. Does your school consistently share student-achievement data? Does your school share grade-level reading percentages, discipline data, attendance rates, and so on in its monthly newsletters, at parent-teacher organization (PTO) meetings, or during principal open houses? Transparency about such data can be very different for many schools, especially schools that have not historically been successful academically. Trust, however, is contingent on transparency. If parent and family involvement and engagement are to increase, schools must develop a culture of trust that extends beyond the building walls.

The Four Critical Questions

Finally, educators working in PLCs constantly work collaboratively to answer the following four critical questions (DuFour et al., 2016).

1. What do we want our students to learn?
2. How will we know when students have learned it?
3. How will we respond when students haven't learned it?
4. How will we extend and enrich the learning for students who have learned it?

In PLCs, asking and responding to these four critical questions in collaborative teams during instructional planning happens automatically and routinely. At Minnieville Elementary, the staff and I considered how we might use these questions to increase parent and family involvement and engagement. What if parents walked into a parent-teacher conference with the answers to these four critical questions? Minnieville Elementary staff believed if both teachers and parents were on the same page with the answers to these critical questions, then the impact would be immense; parents and families would have a stronger understanding of the roles the teacher and they themselves would need to play to support and assist their children's learning.

PARENT *voices*

You can tell a lot about a school and its community from what you can find on the internet. Of course, you don't want to just look at the reviews and star ratings; yes, those things are important, but an awesome school community goes beyond test scores. As both a parent and a teacher looking for a new teaching position, I wanted to be part of a school community that had an emphasis on family involvement. After researching and having conversations with Principal Provencio, I could tell that Minnieville Elementary had a very clear focus on family involvement and there was a sense of collective responsibility for students. Parental involvement isn't just a buzz word at Minnieville; it is something that is valued by staff members and is a large part of the school's success. Once I began teaching at Minnieville, it became even more evident that Minnieville's mission and vision rang true for all stakeholders. The PLC structure at Minnieville is clear to both parents and teachers. I worked at schools that didn't have a PLC culture, and the difference is palpable. Making the decision to both work at Minnieville and send my child to Minnieville was the best decision I could have made. —S. Baldwin, Minnieville Elementary parent and teacher (personal communication, October 3, 2017)

Final Thoughts

Building parent and family involvement and engagement is not a new topic in education. In fact, the Every Student Succeeds Act (ESSA, 2015) outlines the mandated elements schools must incorporate to foster parent and family engagement. ESSA states that every district must use at least one percent of its Title I funds for parent and family engagement activities, with 90 percent of the funds distributed to schools, with priority given to high-need schools. ESSA also requires that parents and family members of low-income students must be included in decisions regarding how engagement funds are spent. Funds must be used for at least one of the following five activities:

1. Supporting schools in training school staff regarding engagement strategies

2. Supporting programs that reach families at home, in the community, and at school

3. Disseminating information on best practices focused on engagement, especially for increasing engagement of economically disadvantaged families

4. Subgranting to schools to collaborate with community-based organizations or businesses that have a track record of improving family engagement

5. Engaging in any other activities that the district believes are appropriate in increasing engagement

Parent and caregiver interest and involvement in their child's academic work can have profound effects on behavioral and academic outcomes. However, some parents face physical, linguistic, emotional, and cultural barriers that disproportionately impact the parents of students who already face additional challenges at school. School and system leaders can organize and invest to lower these barriers to better engage with parents (Travers, 2018).

At Minnieville Elementary, we use elements of the PLC process to enhance parent, family, and community engagement with great success. I hope our unique outlook and perspective on this vital topic serve you, your school, and your community well. The next chapter discusses our first step in applying PLC elements to boost parent and family involvement and engagement: creating a family-engagement guiding coalition.

Next Steps

One of the most important activities we engaged in at Minnieville during our PLC transformation was to honestly assess where we felt we were as a staff in our understanding of the PLC process. A powerful tool school leaders can utilize for this purpose is "The Professional Learning Communities at Work Continuum: Laying the Foundation" and the "Where Do We Go From Here? Worksheet" (DuFour et al., 2016). This tool appears on the following pages as the Next Steps Tool for chapter 1. Once your school has ascertained where the school community is in its understanding and implementation of the main aspects of the PLC process, work closely with the leadership team to reflect on what PLC areas are solid and which areas are growing and answer the questions in the "Where Do We Go From Here? Worksheet." If efforts to grow as a school with parent and family engagement are a priority, then the information in the chapters that follow will give you a clear road map for how your school can be successful and what tools and resources you will need.

Next Steps Tool for Chapter 1

The Professional Learning Communities at Work® Continuum: Laying the Foundation

Directions: Individually, silently, and honestly assess the current reality of your school's implementation of each indicator listed in the left column. Consider what evidence or anecdotes support your assessment. This form may also be used to assess district or team implementation.

We have a clear sense of our collective purpose, the school we are attempting to create to achieve that purpose, the commitments we must make and honor to become that school, and the specific goals that will help monitor our progress.

Indicator	Pre-Initiating	Initiating	Implementing	Developing	Sustaining
Shared Mission It is evident that learning for all is our core purpose.	The purpose of the school has not been articulated. Most staff members view the mission of the school as teaching. They operate from the assumption that although all students should have the opportunity to learn, responsibility for learning belongs to the individual student and will be determined by his or her ability and effort.	An attempt has been made to clarify the purpose of the school through the development of a formal mission statement. Few people were involved in its creation. It does little to impact professional practice or the assumptions behind those practices.	A process has been initiated to provide greater focus and clarity regarding the mission of learning for all. Steps are being taken to clarify what, specifically, students are to learn and to monitor their learning. Some teachers are concerned that these efforts will deprive them of academic freedom.	Teachers are beginning to see evidence of the benefits of clearly established expectations for student learning and systematic processes to monitor student learning. They are becoming more analytical in assessing the evidence of student learning and are looking for ways to become more effective in assessing student learning and providing instruction to enhance student learning.	Staff members are committed to helping all students learn. They demonstrate that commitment by working collaboratively to clarify what students are to learn in each unit, creating frequent common formative assessments to monitor each student's learning on an ongoing basis, and implementing a systematic plan of intervention when students experience difficulty. They are willing to examine all practices and procedures in light of their impact on learning.

continued ▲

page 1 of 4

Indicator	Pre-Initiating	Initiating	Implementing	Developing	Sustaining
Shared Vision We have a shared understanding of and commitment to the school we are attempting to create.	No effort has been made to engage staff in describing the preferred conditions for the school.	A formal vision statement has been created for the school, but most staff members are unaware of it.	Staff members have participated in a process to clarify the school they are trying to create, and leadership calls attention to the resulting vision statement on a regular basis. Many staff members question the relevance of the vision statement, and their behavior is generally unaffected by it.	Staff members have worked together to describe the school they are trying to create. They have endorsed this general description and use it to guide their school-improvement efforts and their professional development.	Staff members can and do routinely articulate the major principles of the school's shared vision and use those principles to guide their day-to-day efforts and decisions. They honestly assess the current reality in their school and continually seek more effective strategies for reducing the discrepancy between that reality and the school they are working to create.
Collective Commitments (Shared Values) We have made commitments to each other regarding how we must behave in order to achieve our shared vision.	Staff members have not yet articulated the attitudes, behaviors, or commitments they are prepared to demonstrate in order to advance the mission of learning for all and the vision of what the school might become.	Administrators or a committee of teachers have created statements of beliefs regarding the school's purpose and its direction. Staff members have reviewed and reacted to those statements. Initial drafts have been amended based on staff feedback. There is no attempt to translate the beliefs into the specific commitments or behaviors that staff will model.	A statement has been developed that articulates the specific commitments staff have been asked to embrace to help the school fulfill its purpose and move closer to its vision. The commitments are stated as behaviors rather than beliefs. Many staff object to specifying these commitments and prefer to focus on what other groups must do to improve the school.	Staff members have been engaged in the process to articulate the collective commitments that will advance the school toward its vision. They endorse the commitments and seek ways to bring them to life in the school.	The collective commitments are embraced by staff, embedded in the school's culture, and evident to observers of the school. They help define the school and what it stands for. Examples of the commitments are shared in stories and celebrations, and people are challenged when they behave in ways that are inconsistent with the collective commitments.

Indicator	Pre-Initiating	Initiating	Implementing	Developing	Sustaining
Common School Goals We have articulated our long-term priorities, short-term targets, and timelines for achieving those targets.	No effort has been made to engage the staff in establishing school-improvement goals related to student learning.	Goals for the school have been established by the administration or school-improvement team as part of the formal district process for school improvement. Most staff would be unable to articulate a goal that has been established for their school.	Staff members have been made aware of the long-term and short-term goals for the school. Tools and strategies have been developed and implemented to monitor the school's progress toward its goals. Little has been done to translate the school goal into meaningful targets for either collaborative teams or individual teachers.	The school goal has been translated into specific goals that directly impact student achievement for each collaborative team. If teams are successful in achieving their goals, the school will achieve its goal as well. Teams are exploring different strategies for achieving their goals.	All staff members pursue measurable goals that are directly linked to the school's goals as part of their routine responsibilities. Teams work interdependently to achieve common goals for which members are mutually accountable. The celebration of the achievement of goals is part of the school culture and an important element in sustaining the PLC process.

Source: DuFour et al., 2016, pp. 47–49.

Where Do We Go From Here? Worksheet
Laying the Foundation

Indicator of a PLC at Work	What steps or activities must be initiated to create this condition in your school?	Who will be responsible for initiating or sustaining these steps or activities?	What is a realistic timeline for each step or phase of the activity?	What will you use to assess the effectiveness of your initiative?
Shared Mission It is evident that learning for all is our core purpose.				
Shared Vision We have a shared understanding of and commitment to the school we are attempting to create.				
Collective Commitments (Shared Values) We have made commitments to each other regarding how we must behave in order to achieve our shared vision.				
Common School Goals We have articulated our long-term priorities, short-term targets, and timelines for achieving those targets.				

Source: DuFour et al., 2016, p. 50.

CHAPTER 2

CREATING A FAMILY-ENGAGEMENT GUIDING COALITION

Teamwork is the ability to work together toward a common vision. The ability to direct individual accomplishments toward organizational objectives. It is the fuel that allows common people to attain uncommon results.

—*Andrew Carnegie*

Leaders of PLCs acknowledge that "no one person will have the energy, expertise, and influence to lead a complex change process . . . without first gaining the support of key staff members" (DuFour et al., 2016, p. 27). The PLC process calls for the creation of a schoolwide *leadership team* or *guiding coalition* because "leaders in all walks of life and all kinds of organizations, public and private, need to depend on others to accomplish the group's purpose" (Wallace Foundation, 2012, as cited in DuFour et al., 2016, p. 27). Thought leader John P. Kotter (2012) in his book *Leading Change* describes a *guiding coalition* as the group of people an organization assembles that has enough power to lead the change and work together as a team.

At Minnieville Elementary, creating guiding coalitions was an essential step in our PLC transformation to help grow our PLC culture and begin turning around student achievement. Teachers were given the opportunity to become a part of a guiding coalition that was best suited for their area of strength as an educator. Guiding coalitions focused on core academic areas, such as mathematics, science, and language arts. In addition, Minnieville created opportunities for teachers to participate in a wellness guiding coalition and a multicultural guiding coalition. Guiding coalitions analyzed data, determined action plans, and sought out and provided resources and professional learning to staff. Both the assistant principal and I played a key role in working with and supporting these guiding coalitions, which met twice a month. Our teams carefully reviewed end-of-year assessment data and determined specific objectives proven to be challenging for teachers and students. The guiding coalitions then used academic data to create *SMART goals* (goals that are specific, measurable, achievable, relevant, and time bound; Conzemius & O'Neill, 2014) to provide attainable and measurable benchmarks to work toward. After a year of doing this work (along with participation in professional learning opportunities to assist teacher growth), Minnieville Elementary student achievement began to rise, and the results were tangible.

Despite this success, as principal, I felt as though I had fallen short of focusing on a key element in our mission of learning for all—learning for *all* adults in our community, and this meant parents, family, and community members. As a school, we were not addressing the needs of our parents and families and focusing on the larger community. Because the staff and I had begun to see success with our academic guiding coalitions, I approached the leadership team and asked members if they felt a family-engagement guiding coalition would be useful. The team agreed, so our teachers that were most interested and passionate about this area began to build a guiding coalition to address the needs of parents, families, and community members.

This chapter covers creating a guiding coalition for family engagement, including choosing the right people, doing the work, determining SMART goals, and uncovering resources.

Choosing the Right People

The first step in creating a family-engagement guiding coalition is to seek the right staff and faculty members to do the work of building and enhancing parent and family engagement in your school. Most teachers are relatively highly skilled in academic instruction, but perhaps not so much in parent and family involvement and engagement.

At Minnieville, teachers could choose which guiding coalition they wanted to be part of. Teachers with strength in mathematics generally gravitated to that guiding coalition; teachers passionate about literacy gravitated toward the language arts guiding coalition. For the family-engagement guiding coalition, the administrative team sought members who were relational, possessed high levels of emotional intelligence, were socially and civically minded, and demonstrated an awareness of cultural diversity. Teachers with these qualities are ideal candidates for this type of team. After announcing the creation of the family-engagement guiding coalition, Minnieville was fortunate to have an outstanding group of teachers volunteer for the team. Ashley Hoyle, a third-grade teacher leader, volunteered to be the team leader.

TEACHER *voices*

Family involvement is an area I have long been passionate about. As a teacher, I did what I could to volunteer for PTO events and help parents whenever possible, but I always felt I could do more to support my school community. I was very excited to learn that my school's administrative team was going to create a family-involvement guiding coalition. I was also thrilled when they asked me if I could serve as the team's leader. Even though I was nervous about this new opportunity, I knew I would have tremendous support from my entire school and our teacher and family volunteers.

Having been a part of other guiding coalitions, I knew that addressing this issue in a collaborative effort could really pay off. I was very excited about collaborating with my team to research successful strategies and methods to increase family engagement, create action items to recruit and train volunteers for our school, and seek out ways to measure and monitor our efforts. —A. Hoyle, Teacher, Minnieville Elementary (personal communication, September 15, 2017)

Doing the Work

In PLCs, collaborative teams always work in cycles of *collective inquiry* (DuFour et al., 2016). This means teams collaboratively engage in action research, focusing on asking and answering the right questions to achieve better results for students. The first meeting for the family-engagement guiding coalition proceeded as follows.

Team members first decided their call to action. A tenet of Minnieville Elementary's vision statement is to focus on our community, so the team needed to ascertain our families' goals and *how* they would quantify those goals as they relate to family involvement and engagement with the school. The team then decided what data to use and what strategies and activities would be necessary to meet the goals. This team's work was unique to Minnieville Elementary, but members were determined to do the right work to support the school's mission and vison.

Collecting Baseline Data

A PLC's family-engagement guiding coalition should first extrapolate data to use as a baseline for measuring the goals members will try to achieve. Teams should utilize any qualitative and quantitative data to assist them in determining how to meet the needs of parents and families. If available, utilize data from the following sources.

- **Parent-school feedback surveys:** District- or school-created surveys are ideal to gather parent perceptions of the level of quality schools have in a multitude of areas. Surveys are available for schools to utilize or adapt, such as the Family-School Relationships Survey by Panorama Education (www.panoramaed.com/family-school-relationships-survey) or the Family Engagement Surveys from the Kansas Parent Information Resource Center (n.d.; Henderson, Mapp, Johnson, & Davies, 2007).

- **Volunteer attendance:** These data show the number of volunteers a school has during the school year in order to reveal trends during months, events, for grade levels, and so on.

- **Visitor attendance:** These data show the number of visitors during a specific timeframe. There are programs and management systems available to support schools with tracking visitor attendance, such as SchoolPass (www.schoolgateguardian.com), teamgo (www.teamgo.co), and Visitu (https://visitu.com).

- **Parent and family attendance at school events:** These data track parent and family attendance at school-related events, such as parent-teacher conferences, fundraising events, informational events, sporting events, school ceremonies, and so on.

- **Facebook, Twitter, and other social media platforms:** These data could include number of followers, likes, or visitors that schools have on their various social media platforms.

The Minnieville Elementary family-engagement guiding coalition began its work by analyzing volunteer attendance data from the previous year to ascertain how many parents, family members, and community volunteers assisted the school. The team retrieved data from a school-based system volunteers and visitors utilize before visiting the school. Most schools have such online systems, which can make data retrieval relatively easy. Some schools, however, may track their volunteers and visitors using sign-in binders found at the school's front office.

When the team began to examine the data, members were shocked to find that in the previous year, there were only forty documented volunteer hours. The team also discovered the school had no social media presence, and family attendance at school-based PTO fundraising functions was relatively low at around 3 percent of the school's total population. Having these baseline data gave the team a clear picture of where we were as a school and where we wanted to go.

Discovering the Barriers

At Minnieville Elementary, the data revealed there was very little parent and family involvement or engagement with the school. The next steps for the family-engagement guiding coalition were to discover the barriers to parent and family participation. Research reveals that schools face many barriers to parent and family engagement. Project Appleseed (n.d.), a national campaign for public school improvement, finds the most common barriers to parent and family engagement are as follows.

- **Lack of teacher time:** Teachers often see working on family involvement as a task added to an already long list of responsibilities (Caplan, 2000).

- **Lack of understanding of parents' communication styles:** Some efforts at increasing involvement fail because there is a mismatch in the communication styles of families and teachers, often due to cultural and language differences (Caplan, 2000; Liontos, 1992).

- **Teachers' misperceptions of parents' abilities:** Some teachers believe parents can't help their children because they have limited educational backgrounds themselves; however, many poorly educated families support learning by talking with their children about school, monitoring homework, and making it clear that education is important and that they expect their children to do well in school (Caplan, 2000).

- **Limited family resources:** Lack of time is the major reason family members identify for why they don't get more involved. Lack of transportation and childcare also keeps families from participating (Caplan, 2000).

- **Parents' lack of comfort:** Some parents feel intimidated and unwelcome at school. Many parents had negative school experiences themselves or are so unfamiliar with the American culture that they do not want to get involved or feel unsure about the value of their contributions. Barriers are also created by parents who have feelings of inadequacy or are suspicious of or angry at the school (Caplan, 2000; Jones, 2001; Liontos, 1992).

- **Tension in relationships between parents and teachers:** Parent and teacher focus groups, conducted around the country as part of the Parents as School Partners research project, identified common areas of conflict between parents and teachers (Baker, 2000).

  - Parents felt that teachers waited too long before telling them about a problem and that they only heard from teachers when there was bad news. Most parents felt they didn't have easy or ongoing access to their children's teachers and that teachers blamed parents when children had problems in school. Some parents felt unwelcome at the school, believed schools didn't really want their input, and thought communication was a one-way system, with schools sending out information and parents having few, if any, opportunities to share ideas with the school.

◆ Teachers believed parents didn't respect them, challenged their authority, and questioned their decisions. They believed parents encouraged students to disrespect them. Teachers resented that not all parents sent their children to school ready to learn and wanted parents to follow through more with the academic and disciplinary suggestions they made.

• **Mobility:** Some urban areas have low rates of home ownership. Families that rent tend to move around a lot more, which makes it harder to build relationships between families and school staff (Metropolitan St. Louis, 2004).

• **Lack of vested interest:** Many families don't see the value in participating and don't believe their involvement will result in any meaningful change (American Association of School Administrators, 1998).

• **Difficulties of involvement in the upper grades:** There is typically less parent involvement at the middle and senior high school levels, as adolescents strive for greater autonomy and separation from their parents. Families often live further from the school their child attends and are less able to spend time there (Caplan, 2000).

With these findings in mind, the Minnieville team held a follow-up meeting where it strategically invited approximately ten parents representing various grade levels and demographics to assist in brainstorming reasons why parents and families were not involved or engaged with the school. The insight and honest conversations these parents offered our team were truly remarkable. These parent members worked side by side with the family-engagement guiding coalition to create a list of roadblocks they felt were keeping parents and families away from the school. The following is a list of the top-ten barriers for Minnieville Elementary.

1. Lack of administration support for family involvement and engagement

2. A few parents making decisions for all parents

3. Lack of translation services for diverse languages

4. Lack of parent availability during and after school hours

5. Lack of transportation to the home and school

6. Lack of parent knowledge and understanding of school-related business

7. Fear of immigration concerns

8. Cultural differences and lack of understanding of school-home relationships

9. Lack of positive customer-service attitude by some school staff members

10. Poor communication about school-based events

This list proved vital for team understanding of *why* so few parents, families, and volunteers had been present in the school. It also showed that much work needed to be done for Minnieville Elementary to become a family-focused school community.

Equipped with the knowledge of how many documented hours parents had been involved with the school and what barriers were preventing involvement and engagement, the next step was for the team to carefully examine their traditional school-based events, functions, and activities in order to understand how attendance and participation could be enhanced for parents and families.

Creating a Parent- and Family-Engagement Survey

One of the most powerful tools a family-engagement guiding coalition can utilize is a school-created survey. As Phil Cleave (2017) shares, the business world has long used customer surveys as a tool to gather information about business practices, customer service, products, and so on. Information gathered from customer satisfaction surveys provides valuable insight for your organization to stay relevant and to understand customer needs and wants. Successful business owners and managers know that it costs more money to attract a new customer than to keep an existing one. It makes sense to retain customers and build a loyal relationship with them so that not only do they return to purchase from you, rather than a competitor, but they become advocates of your brand.

The survey can be informal or formal; use the survey to ascertain how parents and families currently feel about the school community, teachers, and administrators; the level of support and resources they are receiving from the school; the quality of education they believe their child is obtaining; the level of communication parents and families receive; and so on. There are several school- and family-engagement surveys available online. One excellent survey schools can access as an exemplar is from the Ohio Department of Education (2009). (This comprehensive parent survey and instructions are available online at www.in.gov/sboe/files/ODE-Family-Involvement -Instructions-and-Survey.pdf.) Because of Minnieville Elementary's focused efforts to integrate family engagement with elements of the PLC process, the team used the survey questions in figure 2.1 (page 26) to assist in obtaining baseline feedback about where the school was with parent- and family-involvement and engagement efforts. The team asked parents and families to respond *yes* or *no* to each question.

Instructions: Please indicate *yes* or *no* for each of the following questions.	Yes	No
1. I know my child's school's vision and mission.		
2. My child's school and teacher clearly communicate schoolwide academic goals and learning targets.		
3. I have access to my child's instructional calendars and pacing guides that outline what my child will be learning.		
4. I can easily access state, county, or division academic standards of learning.		
5. I receive clear and concise communication about my child's academic and behavioral progress.		
6. I receive clear and concise communication about all school-related events.		
7. My child's teacher explains the instructional resources and strategies that he or she will use to help my child learn.		
8. My child's teacher has explained the instructional resources and strategies that he or she will use if my child has not learned the standard.		
9. My child's teacher explains the instructional resources and strategies that he or she will use if my child has mastered the standard.		
10. My child's school building is well kept and appealing both inside and outside.		
11. I feel welcome when I enter my child's school.		
12. I have access to strategies, resources, and materials to assist me with my child's learning.		
13. My child's school invites me to be an active participant in the decision-making process of the school.		
14. There are many ways I can be involved in my child's school.		
15. I am a valued participant and partner in my child's success as a learner.		
16. I am informed of community-based resources and supports (adult education opportunities, language services, job opportunities, health support, mental health resources, utilities, and so on).		

Source: © 2016 by Minnieville Elementary School. Used with permission.

Figure 2.1: Sample parent- and family-engagement survey.

*Visit **go.SolutionTree.com/PLCbooks** for a free reproducible version of this figure.*

Determining SMART Goals

Now that the family-engagement guiding coalition understands why a school lacks parent and family involvement and engagement, it is time to set goals for improvement. PLCs set *SMART goals* or goals that are specific, measurable, achievable, relevant, and time bound (Conzemius & O'Neill, 2014).

- **Specific:** Well-defined, clear, and unambiguous

- **Measurable:** With specific criteria that measure your progress toward the accomplishment of the goal

- **Achievable:** Attainable and not impossible to achieve

- **Relevant:** Realistic and fitting to your purpose

- **Time bound:** With a clearly defined timeline, including a starting date and a target date

In the first year, Minnieville Elementary's SMART goal for parent and family involvement and engagement was as follows.

As measured by parent and visitor volunteer hours, our school will raise its overall family participation rate to four hundred hours by June 2013.

During the first year, the team created a list of six specific actions to assist in meeting this goal. It was very important to our family-engagement guiding coalition to create tangible activities to begin building momentum toward the goal of increasing both parent involvement and engagement. The team settled on these first six actions because they are areas the school has the capacity to address with the resources available.

1. Create a parent and family survey to assist in the school's customer-service efforts (shown in figure 2.1). It was vital for the team to create and utilize a school-based survey to collect baseline data about parent and family perception of our customer-service efforts.

2. Actively recruit parents and family members to assist with supporting teachers and students. Minnieville sought out parents and family members who had the time and resources to come into the school during the school day to assist teachers with various clerical duties, assist in the cafeteria during student lunch times, assist with recess activities for students, volunteer in the school library, and so on.

3. Host mother-, father-, and grandparent-specific events throughout the year. These events highlight the value the school places on parents and families as partners. These events should provide time for family members to come into the school, spend time with their child and their

child's teacher and administration, and obtain information on the school and programs and resources that could help their child.

4. Host a schoolwide multicultural event. At Minnieville, this event was a starting point for our school to recognize and celebrate the immense diversity of our students and families. Families come into the school during an evening to celebrate and share aspects of their country of origin.

5. Seek and maintain business partners. This activity set the stage for Minnieville to begin seeking out and utilizing the support of our business community. The family-engagement guiding coalition sought out potential business partners that could work to support the school by providing resources and volunteers to support student instruction and school events.

6. Ensure all communications to parents are in both English and Spanish. Due to Minnieville's large Latinx community, increasing the school's communication efforts in Spanish was immensely important in ensuring parents were receiving communication consistently and routinely. Minnieville utilizes a myriad of resources to assist in this effort, including bilingual translators, interpreters, and translation software. Having a professional or professionally trained interpreter present addresses this issue by giving parents exactly the information they need in a manner that is easily understood. It also gives parents real-time access to replying or participating in the discussion.

At Minnieville, these six actions, although small changes, provided the quick wins needed to help the school meet its parent- and family-engagement goal. At the end of the first year of implementation, the team smashed its original goal of raising parent and family involvement and engagement to four hundred hours. By June, Minnieville Elementary parents and families had logged more than one thousand hours of involvement and engagement! The difference was remarkable. Because of the team's efforts and the priority members placed on raising parent and family engagement, parents and families began to freely come to the school and ask for ways to volunteer. Attendance at PTO events increased as well, as did attendance at parent-teacher conferences and essential academic meetings. The work of the family-engagement guiding coalition was paying off; however, much work was still needed. Each subsequent year, the team implemented additional strategies based on the previous year's work and school and community needs.

After that first year, the family-engagement guiding coalition developed strategies to actively recruit parents to become more involved in key decisions. The team sought parent leaders to help recruit additional parents and families from their respective cultures and neighborhoods to become parent volunteers at our school. The team then utilized ongoing data to create additional SMART goals to help guide its work. These subsequent family-engagement SMART goals built on the initial success of the family-engagement guiding coalition to continue that momentum. The team felt that enhancing the school's social media presence would be a key next step as well as increase attendance at parent-teacher conferences. Those SMART goals were as follows.

- *By June 2021, the number of families and parents that follow us on Facebook or Twitter will increase by 20 percent.*

- *Attendance rates for parent and family attendance at school conferences will increase by 40 percent.*

As a PLC, Minnieville Elementary staff used the same cycle of continuous improvement, data analysis, and decision making to continually set goals, evaluate data, determine next steps, and evaluate outcomes. This is the same process members use in their grade-level or course-based teams in PLCs.

The family-engagement guiding coalition is also tasked with uncovering and providing resources for parents and families.

Uncovering Resources

As a Title I school, Minnieville leadership never had a problem acquiring adequate instructional resources for teachers and students; it's been relatively well funded through federal, state, and local revenue streams. As our efforts to build stronger partnerships with parents and families increased, Minnieville's family-engagement guiding coalition sought to provide more resources for families, and staff began to learn more about the day-to-day needs and struggles many families experienced. Financial hardships and lack of resources are a major factor keeping many families from being actively involved in their child's school activities. For example, lack of financial resources has an impact on childcare, transportation, time spent in the school, and time spent supporting academic work at home. Lack of time is the major reason given by family members for why they don't get more involved (Caplan, 2000). The school's family-engagement guiding coalition began working to seek out and discover resources to assist families with their child's learning. Through conversations with parents and families, we found two main areas of opportunity where our school could provide resources for parents, families, and students: (1) providing free school supplies for all students and (2) providing technology resources to families in need.

1. Provide free school supplies to all students at the start of the year.
   The idea of providing free school supplies to all students came from
   an embarrassing situation I encountered with a parent when I was
   school-supply shopping for my own children. While in the checkout
   line, I commented about how expensive school shopping is after you
   add up school supplies, clothes, backpacks, and so on. A woman who
   was standing next to me in line heard me saying this and joined the
   conversation, saying she was shopping for her two boys and that the
   school's supply list where they attend is outrageous. She shared that
   they had just moved to the area and her sons were going to Minnieville
   Elementary. "Had I ever heard of it?" she asked. Extremely embarrassed,
   I said I was the principal. I invited her to come to our school and meet
   with our family-engagement guiding coalition.

   From that experience, I vowed to provide a high level of equitability
   for students by carefully utilizing school funds and donations from
   business partners to pay for students' school supplies each year (Palermo,
   2017). The staff and I knew doing so would be a wow factor for our
   families. Each year, our parents and families are overjoyed to learn the
   school is providing all their children's supplies. Some parents enjoy the
   experience of school-supply shopping with their child and ask if they
   can still do this. Of course! We just want to make sure all students and
   families start the year on a level playing field and have a sense of equity.
   As a school, Minnieville makes budgetary decisions to allow us to
   purchase these school supplies every year; however, not all schools have
   resources or opportunity to provide school supplies to all students. I
   strongly encourage school leaders to seek out creative solutions to assist
   students and families with school supplies, such as partnering with local
   businesses or having a community school supply drive.

2. Provide school-based access to technology for family use. At Minnieville,
   we discovered from our interactions with both families and students that
   digital equity was a tremendous area of concern. Many parents simply did
   not have access to computers or the Wi-Fi support their child's learning.
   If parents and families did have this technology, many did not have a
   level of understanding on how to leverage the technology to support
   learning. To address this, the family-engagement guiding coalition
   partnered with the Virginia STAR Initiative. The Virginia Student
   Training and Refurbishment program (Virginia STAR or VA STAR) is
   a statewide program that teaches students to refurbish surplus computer
   hardware from government agencies and private companies. The
   refurbished computers are donated to families, organizations, and school

districts in need. Through participation in the program, students work toward earning industry-standard certifications from companies such as CompTIA, Cisco, Microsoft, and Oracle (Virginia STAR, 2016). In coordination with the school's counseling department, parents receive free laptops and desktops through the Virginia STAR program. Minnieville also partners with a local cable provider to provide families with Wi-Fi access at a reduced cost. In addition to providing technology to the most in-need families, the school provides lessons and tutorials to assist families with how to set up, navigate, and manage their new technology.

Some other support services Minnieville has provided include access to free English language classes to parents, access to immigration attorneys once a year, flexible locations for school-based parent-teacher meetings, and opportunities to meet with local law enforcement to address community needs.

Each year at Minnieville Elementary, parent and family volunteer hours increased, as table 2.1 shows. By 2019, our school had over six thousand hours of parent, family, and visitor involvement and engagement. For a school with a population of over 80 percent economically disadvantaged and 75 percent second-language learners, this was remarkable. As parent involvement grew, so did students' academic achievement scores. Table 2.1 also shows that Minnieville Elementary's statewide ranking increased from 23 percent in 2011 to 85 percent in 2019 (Minnieville Elementary, n.d.). Parents and families were much more invested in the academic success of both their children and their neighborhood school—and had a renewed sense of pride in the accomplishments of the school and in the school's efforts to better support parent and family engagement.

Table 2.1: Volunteer Hours and Academic Ranking 2011–2019

Year	Number of Volunteer Hours	Virginia Statewide Ranking
2011	450	23 percent
2012	1,944	40 percent
2013	2,434	60 percent
2014	2,982	82 percent
2015	4,459	73 percent
2016	4,515	74 percent
2017	5,056	53 percent
2018	5,500	83 percent
2019	6,123	85 percent

Source: Minnieville Elementary, n.d.

Final Thoughts

Strong PLC cultures utilize guiding coalitions to help do the work of school improvement. Guiding coalitions constantly conduct action research, collect and analyze data, set goals, and create strategies to help grow their efforts to achieve those goals. Just like schools would utilize a guiding coalition to help address student mathematics or literacy needs, Minnieville Elementary utilized this approach to increase and enhance parent- and family-engagement efforts. Our school saw a direct correlation between academic achievement growth and parent and family engagement.

Next Steps

We found that utilizing the power of a guiding coalition to address parent and family involvement and engagement is key to a school's growth. Along with your team of teachers, administrators, and parent volunteers, consider the questions in the reproducible "Next Steps Tool for Chapter 2" to help guide your work in this effort.

Next Steps Tool for Chapter 2

1. Which school and district staff members and parents will be key players in our family-engagement guiding coalition?

2. What data will we use to collect as a baseline for our goal-setting efforts?

3. What do our data currently tell us about our family involvement and engagement efforts in our school?

4. How does our school define a volunteer?

5. What are some current obstacles and barriers that prohibit more involved and engaged parents?

6. What events and opportunities does our school currently provide for our parents and families?

7. What specific activities, strategies, and resources could our school provide to help increase parent, family, and community involvement and engagement?

8. What SMART goals could we create to help guide our work in raising parent and family involvement and engagement?

CHAPTER 3

ARTICULATING A FAMILY-FOCUSED MISSION AND VISION

*The most deeply motivated people—not to mention
those who are the most productive and satisfied—hitch their
desires to a cause larger than themselves. . . . Nothing bonds
a team like a shared mission. The more people that share
a common cause . . . the more your group will do deeply
satisfying and outstanding work.*

—Daniel H. Pink

People like Martin Luther King Jr., Steve Jobs, and the Wright brothers may seem to have little in common, but they all started with the why. They realized that people won't truly buy into a product, service, movement, or idea until they understand the why behind it (Sinek, 2009). Take a moment to consider some of the biggest companies in the world. I bet if someone asked you what Nike's slogan is, you would say, "Just do it"; this slogan is one of the most recognizable in the business world. Yet, at the end of the day, the Nike company makes and sells shoes. The shoes they sell may be incredibly awesome, but they don't actually make you a better athlete or teammate. The official mission statement for Nike is to "Bring inspiration and innovation to every athlete in the world" (Nike, n.d.). However, we immediately recognize their slogan as, "Just do it." Can you imagine if your school's mission statement and slogan were as recognizable as Nike's? To me, a school's academic mission is much more important than a shoe company's, yet in our schools, I have found that most parents and families do not have any idea of what their school's vision and mission actually are.

Every successful organization has a strong vision and mission. Consider the following mission and vision statements from four very successful organizations.

- Walmart's vision is, "To be the destination for customers to save money, no matter how they want to shop." Its mission is, "To save people money so they can live better" (Ferguson, 2019).

- McDonald's vision is, "To move with velocity to drive profitable growth and become an even better McDonald's serving more customers delicious food each day around the world." Its mission is, "To be our customer's favorite place and way to eat and drink" (Meyer, 2019).

- Southwest Airlines' vision is, "To be the world's most loved, most flown, and most profitable airline." Its mission is, "Dedication to the highest quality of customer service delivered with a sense of warmth, friendliness, individual pride, and company spirit" (Evans, 2019).

- Apple's vision is, "We believe that we are on the face of the Earth to make great products and that's not changing." Its mission is, "Bringing the best user experience to customers through innovative hardware, software, and services" (Rowland, 2019).

Now think about your school. On the count of three, say your mission and vision statements aloud. Ready? 1 . . . 2 . . . 3 . . . . Did you say them? If you did, you are awesome and so is your school. I ask principals and teachers this question often and, unbelievably, most of the time staff have no idea. Think about this: Why is it that we know more about a shoe company or a fast food restaurant than we do about the most important organization a community has—its school?

Collaboratively creating and articulating your school's mission and vision are among the most vital elements for a school community beginning its PLC journey. Your mission and vision must become your Nike slogan—they must be synonymous with your school; in Lewis Carroll's (1865) *Alice's Adventures in Wonderland*, the Cheshire Cat expresses the sentiment, "If you don't know where you are going, any road will take you there." This saying perfectly articulates the rationale for *why* schools must have a strong and consistent vision and mission. Regardless of whether you're running a small one-person operation, a large corporation, or a school, a mission and vision help provide employees with a purpose. The mission and vision of an organization define future goals and how to get there (Ahmed, 2019). The mission and vision are like the North Star a school community should follow on the journey to achieving its goals.

In 2010 when I joined Minnieville Elementary as the new principal, I tried to find out all I could about the school. I went to the school's website to find the mission and vision statements. To my surprise, I did find them. The mission was a lengthy statement that covered virtually every aspect of the school from instruction to behavior:

> At Minnieville, we will work hard every day to make sure all of our students achieve high levels of performance and conduct themselves as exemplary citizens. Teachers and staff will come to school prepared with exemplary lessons, activities, and strategies that best meet the diverse academic needs for our student population and challenge students to learn and achieve at a higher level. Teachers and staff will conduct themselves as professionals and will be role models for each other, the students, and the community.

The school's vision was "Soaring for Excellence."

At the time, I questioned whether staff members actually knew this mission statement, and, better yet, Did any parents and family members know it? Not surprisingly, virtually no one did. This was a huge problem. How can a school achieve its goals without staff knowing its destination or the actions they should take to get there? It also occurred to me that even though the school had a comprehensive mission, no one knew it because staff and parents were not involved in its creation. Creating the school's mission statement was more of an administrative task to check off a list than a collaborative effort that brought stakeholders together to articulate the main purpose of the school. And administrators did not share the school's vision and mission; because of this, I knew we as administrators, along with both teachers and parents, would have to start from scratch and collaboratively formulate a new shared vision and mission.

This chapter examines involving parents and family members in the process of implementing norms, creating or refining the mission and vision.

Involving Parents and Family Members

If looking to involve parents and families in the process of creating or refining the school's vision and mission statements, school leaders must actively seek out and recruit those parents who represent a wide sample of stakeholders. These stakeholders must represent a wide range of the school community. Doing so will create strong buy-in and ownership. It's important to not just invite the parents who visit the building the most. Call, text, or invite parents (in person during student pick-up time, at bus stops, or at sporting events, and so on) to be a part of this process. During your day-to-day interactions with your school community, be on the lookout for parents and family members who may have a unique voice and perspective to assist with tasks like creating or refining a school's mission and vision. Remember, without parent participation and commitment, there is no buy-in or ownership, so working to involve a diverse and representative parent-school team to assist in this process is vital. In addition to your family-engagement guiding coalition, be sure to invite staff, teachers, and assistants to support this work. Explain to parents and families and the participants that you are inviting them to be a part of a vital school-based team that will be working to create pillars (mission and vision) for the school for years to come. In my experience, parents and families are thrilled to be part of such important work.

Implementing Norms

Once you, as school leader, have worked to establish and support a team to create or refine your school's mission and vision, support the team in establishing team norms to help guide the work. As Mike Mattos and his coauthors (2016) note:

> Norms are ground rules and habits that govern the group. When individuals work through a process to create explicitly shared norms, and then commit to honor those norms, they increase the likelihood they will begin to function as a collaborative team rather than a loose collection of people working together. (p. 72)

Team norms are not intended to serve as rules, but rather as collective commitments—public agreements shared among the members (Kegan & Lahey, 2001). For some parents, being a part of a major collaborative school action is a very foreign concept, while others might be very comfortable with it. Create team norms and build consensus to honor every participant's voice and opinion about the creation or refinement of the school's mission and vision. The team's norms should define how each participant will act and behave while participating in the group, and establish timelines and goals for the work and pragmatics for how members will accomplish the work. Although it is important for school leaders not to create norms in advance for teams, I have found that providing examples of norms may help teams understand the task of creating norms. Some sample norms to assist a team in guiding their work follow.

- As a team, we will do our part individually and collectively to ensure our task of creating our school's mission and vision is carried out.

- We will honor and respect the opinions and perspectives of all team members as we work to create our school's mission and vision.

- We will work to establish and meet all deadlines in our goal of creating our school's mission and vision.

In my work as a school leader, I have found that when teams are creating norms to guide their work, less is more. Teams should review and discuss norms at the start of each meeting and be open to discuss if any barriers or obstacles are interfering with the team's purpose. When done well, norms can help establish trust, openness, commitment, and accountability that move teams from the trivial to the substantive (Blanchard, 2007).

Creating or Refining the Mission and Vision

One tool that may assist team members in their work to create or refine a mission and vision is an affinity diagram. An *affinity diagram* is a tool that gathers participants' ideas and opinions and organizes them into groupings based on their relationships. As author Margaret A. Byrnes (2012) outlines in her book *There Is Another Way!*, the affinity diagram process uses ideas a group generates by brainstorming; this is a good way to get people to work creatively to address difficult issues. Use an affinity diagram in situations the team has not previously explored or when circumstances are confusing or disorganized, such as when people with diverse experiences form a new team, or when members have incomplete knowledge of the area of analysis. When teams utilize an affinity diagram model, participants first brainstorm ideas based on a question. Figure 3.1 shows the basic structure of an affinity diagram. The team would follow the same process to help create the school's mission.

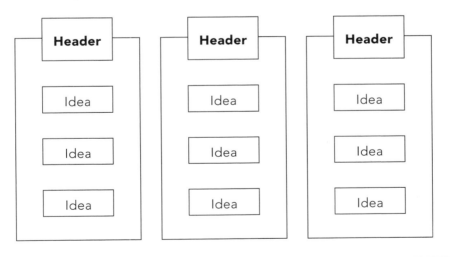

Figure 3.1: Affinity diagram for mission and vision creation.

For example, to create a vision for the school, participants should take the following four steps.

1. Using note cards, participants write down thoughts and ideas about what type of school organization they would like to see in the future.

2. Participants display their ideas on a large table for the entire group to see.

3. The team sorts the ideas into groups based on similarities and generates a title or heading for each.

4. The team collaborates to create a final topic statement that synthesizes a vision statement based on the headings.

Once the team revises or creates working school mission and vision statements, it is vital to then share drafts with all teachers, parents, and even students for feedback and consensus. Once the school principal or group facilitator compiles and revises the feedback and suggestions, the school's mission and vision are ready for communication and promotion to students' families and the community. Figure 3.2 shows a sample affinity diagram that shows the work of a team creating a draft of a school's mission and vision.

At Minnieville Elementary, parents who helped collaboratively create our mission and vision were overjoyed with the process and extremely thankful for having the opportunity to assist. These parents became key ambassadors in helping their neighbors and friends understand what our school was trying to become. They became

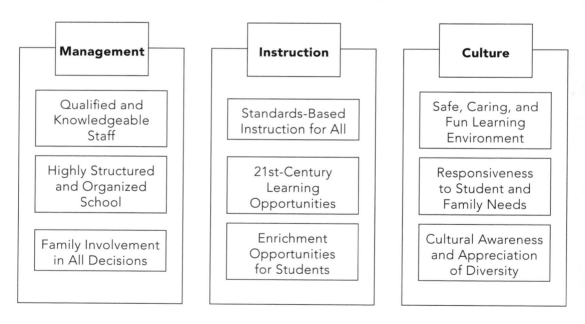

Figure 3.2: Sample affinity diagram for mission and vision creation.

strong advocates who would later serve as key members on parent-teacher advisory councils and PTOs for years to come simply because they were actively involved in the creation of the school mission and vision.

Your school's mission and vision should become part of your staff's everyday language and provide insight into how your school does business. Your school should articulate them in newsletters, in announcements, on websites, and via social media platforms. For example, at Minnieville Elementary, when the school interviews new-teacher candidates, all interview questions reflect the school's mission statement. When the school- and parent-advisory council is deciding how to allocate funds, the team will ask if the purchases will enhance and promote the school's mission and vision. When the PTO seeks to create a program or start a fundraising effort, members make sure their decisions align to the school's mission and vision. Staying consistent helps Minnieville Elementary staff stay focused on what is truly essential in the day-to-day operation of the school.

Ensuring school stakeholders know and understand the mission and vision will not happen overnight. At Minnieville Elementary, after more than eight years of communicating, staff are still not 100 percent sure all stakeholders (including teachers, staff, students, parents, and community members) can articulate our school's mission and vision. We are, however, much further along on our journey, and the steps taken to advance and promote our foundational purpose have truly been rewarding.

Final Thoughts

Consider your organization's mission and vision. They are more than just slogans; they form a contract explaining how each stakeholder in your school will act and behave, plus they clearly define what the school is trying to become and achieve. Parents and families are essential in a school's efforts to grow students' academic achievement; they must play a role in the creation or refinement and articulation of the vision and mission. For a school to grow as an organization and as a PLC, all stakeholders must buy into and understand the mission and vision. Doing this will greatly strengthen the school's culture.

Next Steps

When looking to either create or refine your school's mission and vision with parent and family involvement, your school should consider the questions in the reproducible "Next Steps Tool for Chapter 3" (page 42). If the answer is *no* to any of the questions, consider which next steps for action are necessary to get a positive response.

Next Steps Tool for Chapter 3

1. Were our school's mission and vision collaboratively created with all stakeholders including parents, students, teachers, and administration?

Yes   No

What next steps should we take?

2. Has a diverse staff and parent group in our school clearly identified the key terms in our mission and vision?

Yes   No

What next steps should we take?

3. Have we worked to ensure all teachers, parents, community members, and students know and understand our mission and vision?

Yes   No

What next steps should we take?

4. Do we actively communicate our mission and vision in all school publications?

Yes   No

What next steps should we take?

5. Do we reference the vision and mission when making key building instructional and financial decisions?

Yes   No

What next steps should we take?

6. Do our parent organizations reference our mission and vision when making key decisions?

Yes   No

What next steps should we take?

CHAPTER 4

ACHIEVING A CUSTOMER-CENTRIC CULTURE

People will forget what you said, people will
forget what you did, but people will never
forget how you made them feel.

—Maya Angelou

Take a minute or two to think about your most amazing dining experience at a restaurant. How did the restaurant look when you pulled up? Were the grounds neat and clean? Was the building well maintained? Was the entrance inviting? Was someone there to welcome you? Were you seated relatively quickly? Was the menu well-organized and easy to read? Was the server polite and attentive? Was the food warm, correctly prepared, and delicious? As someone who loves food and enjoys going to restaurants, I am extremely appreciative of amazing customer service. One can find examples of excellent customer service throughout the retail and hospitality industries. These establishments train their employees to be experts in the art of customer service because not doing so would significantly hurt their profit margins. Creating amazing customer-service experiences is commonplace in the business world. Now let's shift gears and think about customer service in public schools.

Even though public schools are nonprofits, the professionals in them do work with myriad customers including students, faculty, parents, families, community members, and other visitors. Despite this, public-school principals and teachers rarely receive training in customer service during their undergraduate or master's programs. Why, if schools serve the academic and social-emotional needs of students and families, would specific training in customer service not be mandatory?

The PLC process does not specifically address customer service in schools. However, the driving force in the PLC process is that the "fundamental purpose of the school is to ensure that all students learn at high levels" (DuFour et al., 2016, p. 11). If parents and families don't like coming to the school and the staff have a reputation of poor customer service, you are probably not going to have students learning at high levels!

In this chapter, I will examine the importance of schools strategically and systematically focusing on a culture of customer service and the customer experience as a means to assist in achieving the fundamental purpose of helping all students learn at high levels. This chapter will focus on four main areas schools may want to consider focusing on to drastically improve their customer service and the customer experience for parents, families, and community members.

1. **Creating first impressions that last a lifetime:** Ensure exemplary customer service begins before parents, families, and visitors arrive at the school door.

2. **Serving families with a smile:** Always make each parent, family member, and visitor feel special when he or she arrives, and remember the customer is always right—as long as you see it from his or her perspective.

3. **Building a wow-factor culture:** Always try to give parents, family members, and visitors more than they expect.

4. **Fostering a doors-open policy:** The principal, assistant principals, deans, and department heads should always be available to address parents' questions and requests without an appointment, while also seeking to provide support for parents and families in their homes.

The sections that follow explain how we developed these four areas of focus at Minnieville Elementary to improve the customer-service experience for parents and families over the course of several years.

Creating First Impressions That Last a Lifetime

In a study of 3,766 students and over 100 classrooms across the United Kingdom, researchers from the University of Salford (cited in Gunn, 2018), found that lighting, paint colors, temperature, and fresh air had the ability to positively impact student learning. Furthermore, classrooms that were well organized, displayed student work, and featured flexible arrangements improved student outcomes.

As a school leader, begin looking into areas where your staff could improve its customer service, and start from the outside in. How can you ensure a parent, family member, or visitor's positive customer-service experience starts before they ever arrive at the door? Perhaps you need to improve your exterior lighting and make modifications to the parking area, such as resurfacing, repainting, or adding visitor and handicapped parking spaces. Perhaps you need to retrain some or all of your school custodians on grounds maintenance. If you have non–English–speaking families, hang signs written in multiple languages to welcome them.

In 2017, Minnieville Elementary restructured the entire entryway of the school to enhance the curb appeal and create a more welcoming entry. As students, parents, families, and visitors enter the school's main lobby, pictures of student artwork adorn the hallways, along with a large painting containing the school's vision and mission. Additionally, a local artist designed a large rendering of the school's mascot. She even let numerous parents and students assist her in the actual painting process! When parents and students walk by that art, they know they had a huge role in creating it. A built-in glass case housing the numerous awards and trophies the school has earned over the years is also part of the front lobby. Student artwork is rotated monthly so parents see their children's work throughout the year. Banners representing various school awards and achievements are proudly displayed as well.

Financial resources may limit what a school can do to update and enhance its visual presence outside and inside the school, so work with what you have. Take the time as a school leader to walk the grounds each morning and look for ways to improve and enhance the optics of the school building. Invite teachers, parents, and families to walk the grounds and seek out ways the school can enhance its curb appeal. Allow the school's custodial team to give input on how they may enhance the school's grounds and structures. Work to provide the training and resources needed for them to adequately carry out their tasks.

Gary Hopkins (2005) in his article in *Education World*, notes that Paul Young, a retired principal of West Elementary School in Lancaster, Ohio, says a welcoming atmosphere starts with the school custodians. Custodians are responsibile for making the outside of the school appealing. Well-tended school grounds are the first things that visitors notice. Signs on the school's marquee welcome parents and provide information. Principal Young comments, "Our hardworking custodial staff makes sure that the school is spotless. We even have students do 'community service' by having them clean up when they 'mess up'" (Hopkins, 2005).

Welcome signs can make a positive impression, too, according to Principal Young (Hopkins, 2005). "A sign that says 'STOP!' in big letters or one that says 'WARNING! All visitors must first report to the front office!' is not very welcoming. Signs at the front entrance should provide directions and instruction, but the language should be welcoming, not offensive."

Include signs that say "Welcome! We are so glad you are here! Please visit our office through the door to your right so that we can assist you." Spruce up the office or waiting areas to make them appealing and comfortable, such as by playing some soft classical music (Hopkins, 2005).

Remember, first impressions last a lifetime. Will the sight of your school building leave a positive first impression?

Serving Families With a Smile

When parents, families, and visitors arrive at your school, ensure your front office staff have the resources and training they need to personally greet and welcome each person and specifically address any questions, needs, or concerns he or she may have in an expeditious, courteous, and friendly manner. There are numerous resources available for staff that deal specifically with how to create cultures of exemplary customer service and engagement (Hubspot, n.d.). Although these books do not specifically deal with customer service in schools, I strongly recommend them as a starting point for growing customer-service mindsets in your school.

- *The Amazement Revolution: Seven Customer Service Strategies to Create an Amazing Customer (and Employee) Experience* (Hyken, 2011). Authored by customer-service thought leader Shep Hyken, this book offers seven practical strategies to improve customer happiness and loyalty, including cultivating partnerships with customers, providing unique membership awards, and building community with customers.

- *The Fred Factor: How Passion in Your Work and Life Can Turn the Ordinary Into the Extraordinary* (Sanborn, 2004). Motivational speaker Mark Sanborn recounts the true story of Fred, the mail carrier who passionately loves his job and genuinely cares about the people he serves. Because of that, he is constantly going the extra mile handling the mail—and sometimes watching over the houses—of the people on his route, treating everyone he meets as a friend. Where others might see delivering mail as monotonous drudgery, Fred sees an opportunity to make a difference in the lives of those he serves.

- *Start With Why: How Great Leaders Inspire Everyone to Take Action* (Sinek, 2009). Simon Sinek's book details how successful leaders can inspire others to rally behind a cause or a mission and achieve it. Sinek believes in the importance of putting the why before the how or the what. By focusing on the why of your customer, you will be able to more effectively navigate conversations to build rapport and trust with them, which will allow you to build a mutually beneficial relationship and inspire their loyalty.

- *The Nordstrom Way to Customer Experience Excellence: Creating a Values-Driven Service Culture* (Spector & Reeves, 2017). Authors Robert Spector and BreAnne O. Reeves write about how Nordstrom department store has set the standard for customer happiness. Key insights include empowering self-motivated employees to go the extra mile to make customers happy, prioritizing ease-of-use for customers across every touchpoint they have with your brand, and always thinking like the customer to build a customer-centric brand on every team and function within your business.

Front office staff should have the necessary resources to offer assistance in a wide variety of languages as well. Because a large majority of Minnieville Elementary parents and families speak Spanish, school staff translated all informational materials into Spanish.

Of course, safety and security are always the priority; however, they shouldn't be obstacles to addressing the needs of parents and visitors to the school. Treat parents and guardians as VIPs—*very important parents*—when they are visiting and volunteering. At Minnieville Elementary, we give them special VIP badges to wear when inside the building. In addition, give parent volunteers access to the school's copy machine, fax machine, and Wi-Fi if needed to assist them with school-related business. When parents and families are enrolling their children, consider ways to make that experience as simple and straightforward as possible. Have a plan in place for parents and families inquiring about your school to get a tour from a staff member or an administrator. Make sure your school's website is always up to date with relevant information about the school and enrollment. Provide sample enrollment paperwork in multiple languages to assist families with the process.

Unfortunately, many parents and family members might not have had the most positive experiences themselves while in school, or they might have experienced negative situations in their child's former school and are skeptical about a new school. In addition, there can be significant cultural differences in schools that may keep them from feeling welcome. The process of schooling can simply overwhelm some parents and families, and they may feel intimidated just walking into the school.

Front office staff should be aware of these circumstances and understand that each interaction, regardless of a parent's or family's past experience or cultural background, is vital in building relationships.

Parents and family members often come to the building or contact the school when attempting to deal with complicated issues, such as grading, testing, bullying, teacher concerns and questions, and so on. The front office staff are the school's first line of defense to address the myriad of concerns parents may have; they are like lighthouses for parents and families, directing them away from their concerns and leading them to the answers they need to support them and their children. There is no doubt that a school's front office staff can make or break the perception of a school. Even when answering phones, front office staff should do the following.

1. Smile—it really does show on the other end of the line!

2. Say, "Thanks for calling (your school name). This is (your name). How may I help you?"

3. Write down the caller's name, phone number, and question or request.

4. Ensure the caller is satisfied at the end of the call. Ask, "Is there anything else I can do for you today?"

Now don't get me wrong; no one is perfect—including front office staff, teachers, and administrators. We all have bad days, especially when dealing with school stakeholders in difficult situations. As school leaders, we've all had experience with extremely challenging parents who can be hostile and angry about situations beyond your control. Oftentimes, issues that deal more with division policy or regulations arise that can anger parents. When someone confronts Minnieville Elementary front office staff with such a situation, they know to say, "Oh my. This sounds like a very important question or concern. Let me get our school principal." Then I (or the assistant principal) try my best to address the situation. My personal goal is that every parent who comes into my office with a frown leaves with a smile. This doesn't mean they always get what they want, but they definitely get a better understanding of their question or concern, are equipped with a plan of action to support themselves and their child, and feel they are leaving with a resolution to their problem. Hiring and training relational-minded and organized school secretaries, front office staff, and teachers can make or break a school; they set the tone for parent and family engagement.

In *Dealing With Difficult Parents*, Todd Whitaker and Douglas J. Fiore (2016) present some helpful tips for teachers, staff, and administrators in resolving parent-school disputes. The authors state, "Rather than trying to understand precisely what it is that makes some parents angry with us, we need to look for ways to deal with their anger for the benefit of our students" (p. 27).

Knowing how to communicate and keep the bond between teacher and family positive is important so parents trust teachers and the school and give them the benefit of the doubt with issues or problems that could arise with their child.

Following are some ways teachers, administrators, and the school should seek to communicate with families (Whitaker & Fiore, 2016).

- **Build trust:** Regularly communicate with parents to build a personal connection. As Whitaker and Fiore (2016) note, "Making a positive impression before we would have to deliver bad news is essential in building trust. It is essential that we build a relationship before we need the relationship" (p. 35).

- **Provide regular newsletters:** Keep parents and families informed; parents and families who are informed are better equipped to play a role in their children's education.

- **Make positive phone calls and send positive emails or letters:** Take opportunities to catch students doing things right and then share what you've observed with parents and families.

- **Listen:** Effective communication isn't one-sided. Learn and cultivate relationships with parents and guardians by listening to their concerns and needs.

- **Celebrate:** Make sure all parents and families feel welcome and safe in the school and as part of their student's classroom. Celebrate what parents and families bring to the learning experience.

Remember the old saying, "The customer is always right"? Well, there is a lot of truth to that, especially in schools. Swiss hotelier César Ritz had a similar slogan stating *le client n'a jamais tort*, which means *the customer is never wrong*. He also famously stated that "If a diner complains about a dish or wine, immediately remove it and replace it, no questions asked" (Sasser, Jones, & Klein, 1999). While this practice may be practical in the hospitality arena, it can be an extremely challenging mindset for many school staff to embrace. Often parents with the best or even misguided intentions may request things that are unreasonable or undoable in a school setting— especially given finite resources. One thing school staff should always remember is, regardless of whether a parent's request for a service or issue is reasonable or not, every parent and family member truly wants the best for his or her child. *Service with a smile* means serving and working to meet the needs of parents and families to meet the needs of students. It also means all issues, concerns, and requests will be taken seriously and the staff will take a collaborative approach with families to address concerns and remedy problems at the school level. After all, in a PLC culture, collaboration is vital. School leaders sustaining their PLC culture understand all stakeholders are part of a collaborative process where staff will take seriously, investigate, and address all input, ideas, suggestions, questions, and concerns.

If school staff functioning in a strong PLC have done an exemplary job of educating parents and families on the school's mission and vision and are always focused on learning, collaboration, and results, then a mutual understanding will exist between the parents and the school.

Building a Wow-Factor Culture

A school's culture refers to "the beliefs, perceptions, relationships, attitudes, and written and unwritten rules that shape and influence every aspect of how a school functions" (Glossary of Education Reform, 2013); it also refers to more tangible elements like "the physical and emotional safety of students, the orderliness of classrooms and public spaces, or the degree to which a school embraces and celebrates racial, ethnic, linguistic, or cultural diversity" (Glossary of Education Reform, 2013). In addition, in a PLC, the school culture is one of collaboration (DuFour et al., 2016). Education expert Jimmy Casas (2017) notes that "if we want to build schools where parents and teachers are fighting to get in instead of out, we must make developing positive school cultures a priority for every school and principal that welcomes children each day."

One area Minnieville Elementary's family-engagement guiding coalition focuses on is school culture, specifically creating experiences for parents and families that produce memories that last a lifetime—experiences with a *wow factor*. Creating experiences to build a *wow-factor culture* is about letting parents, families, and visitors know that when they enter Minnieville Elementary, something magical is going to happen.

The following sections describe some ways Minnieville builds a wow-factor culture, including school registration, creating relationship-building activities, and planning for special events.

School Registration Fun

School staff should work to create wow-factor experiences from the start of the school year. At Minnieville Elementary, we create these experiences during kindergarten (or any grade) registration since it is the first time many parents and families will enter the school. For this event, Minnieville Elementary staff roll out a red carpet for new families; we play music, have games for students, provide free books for families, hand out organized registration packets in multiple languages, have translators available, and have staff ready to give tours of the building. A goal for these types of events is to get it right first so we don't have to get it right later.

Relationship-Building Activities

By seeking wow-factor opportunities for your school, you are also creating opportunities to build relationships among staff and families. For example, in lieu of traditional all-staff meetings at the start of the year, Minnieville Elementary hosts an *Amazing Race*–style event (Doganieri & van Munster, 2001). This event provides new and current staff members a fun opportunity to collaboratively work on a project that builds collegial spirit, contributes to the community, and helps the staff get to know students, families, and the school's neighborhoods a little bit better. Here's how it works: the first part involves tasks and puzzles for teams of staff members to complete in the school building—for example, locating objects or places around the building based on clues. After racing through the school, the teams go into the Minnieville Elementary community to complete *missions*, which consist of staff members driving to preselected homes so they can learn firsthand about the entire Minnieville Elementary community from valued parents and families.

Staff members get to know community members and the neighborhood through interviews with parents, grandparents, school board members, and community members (about three or four people) who can speak about Minnieville Elementary. Questions cover topics such as, How would you explain your relationship with the school? What makes a great school? What are your hopes for your child during this school year?

Next, staff members must find specific sites in the neighborhoods where the school's families live, such as places of worship, restaurants, grocery stores, drugstores, places for recreation, and libraries. At the last stop on the race, teams receive their final mission, and the race culminates with teachers driving to student homes, welcoming them back to school, and delivering area-business donated school supplies.

Another relationship-building activity is when Minnieville Elementary staff provide direct assistance to parents and families. For example, through Title I family surveys, we determined how the school could best support students' academics at home. Many families stated they needed assistance in setting up a designated space for their child to complete schoolwork. Through generous donations from area business partners, we purchased wooden bookcases, learning station materials, and school supplies for selected Minnieville Elementary families. After grade-level and instructional teams assembled the learning stations, team members delivered them (along with backpacks and other supplies) to the families' homes. Not only does this activity provide families with much-needed resources and supplies, it also gives teachers an important perspective on the areas in which parents and families live and provides the opportunity to build relationships with them.

Special Events

Throughout the year, Minnieville Elementary hosts special events that bring in parents, families, and community members. All guiding coalitions, including our mathematics, literacy, family-engagement teams, and PTOs, create special events to both enhance student learning and foster a sense of community. At the beginning of each year, teams create a master calendar of all major events using the categories of fundraising; student and parent learning; parent and family involvement; and staff, parent, and community engagement. Figure 4.1 shows an event calendar with some of our more successful before- and after-school events that support a wow-factor culture.

Minnieville Elementary Event Calendar				
Month	Fundraising	Student and Parent Learning	Parent and Family Involvement	Staff, Parent, and Family Engagement
August			Books and Pops Community Meet and Greet	The Amazing Race
September			Grandparents Day	School Open House Principal and Advisory Council Meeting
October	Fall Festival		Family Fitness Day	ESOL Family Partner Program Meeting
November		Title I Mathematics and Literacy Night	Family Thanksgiving Event	ESOL Family Partner Program Meeting
December	Minnieville Community 5K	Books and Blankets	Winter Festival Event	Donuts With Dads, Muffins With Moms ESOL Family Partner Program Meeting

January		Student-Led Conferences		Principal and Advisory Council Meeting / ESOL Family Partner Program
February	Valentine's Day Dance			ESOL Community-Engagement Event
March		Title I Mathematics and Literacy Night	Multicultural Celebration	
April	Spring Fling	End-of-Year Testing Parent Information Night		Principal and Advisory Council Meeting
May				
June			Kindergarten Promotion / Fifth-Grade Graduation	Principal and Advisory Council Meeting

Source: © 2017 by Minnieville Elementary. Used with permission.

Figure 4.1: Minnieville Elementary event calendar.

Members of the family-engagement guiding coalition, academic teams, and the school's PTOs collaboratively create these events. The teams design each event with a wow factor to help create a sense of community in the school. Each event also utilizes a host of volunteers, business partners, and school staff to make them special for students and families. Some events are set up as fundraisers, some to focus specifically on student learning, and others to celebrate the great work our students, parents, and families do each day.

As a school leader, however, keep in mind that although school events are excellent ways to build community involvement and engagement and build a wow-factor culture, they can be extremely time consuming to plan and implement, and take many resources to carry out effectively. Minnieville Elementary's family-engagement guiding coalition discovered that when planning for family and community events, they needed to do the following.

1. Strategically schedule and plan for events ahead of time.

2. Seek out volunteers and funding from community organizations and local businesses.

3. Utilize school newsletters, social media, texts, and other means of communication to promote the events.

Fostering a Doors-Open Policy

I always communicated to teachers and staff that they can come to me any time with anything because I have an open-door policy; however, being accessible to staff is different from being visible and approachable to parents and families. Principals might often seek to be accessible to staff, but they must also take steps to be visible and approachable to members of the community. A principal's visibility assures students that there is someone in charge, someone to whom they can go if they are experiencing difficulty, someone they can trust. Being less than highly visible erodes a school's climate and may have students wondering if the school really has a principal. Practicing being approachable and visible can easily be woven into the principal's daily schedule (Ruder, 2006).

As a principal, one of the most important times of my day was to greet each student and family in the morning. This time allowed me to greet students and families each day, touch base with the families, and answer any questions they may have had. This is a positive routine. I began to think, however, about how accessible I was for parents and families at other times. After all, they had to schedule appointments with me. I realized this was hypocritical of me as a leader. If I view parents and families as key members of our PLC, they too should be able to come to me for anything at any time—not just in the morning. As I continued my work with our family-engagement guiding coalition, we agreed that as the school leaders, the assistant principal and I would always be available to parents and visitors when they were in need of assistance. Having a *doors-open policy* for your school simply means parents do not have to schedule meetings if they have a question or concern.

At first, this policy was a huge change for me because the day-to-day business of schooling can be very time consuming. I always want to make sure I am focusing on the right work for teachers and students every day and try very hard to limit distractions that can interfere with the school's vision and mission. Being available for families and parents, however, will eventually help achieve our goal of learning for all. Meeting the needs of parents and families will help them become stronger advocates for your school, teachers, and their own children. At Minnieville Elementary, when a parent comes into the school, he or she knows I will be available to address any question or concern *that day*, even if the parent may have to wait a bit. Listening to and actively collaborating with them as soon as possible show parents and families that the staff and I do care about them and are willing to go the extra mile to support them and their children.

In addition, as a school leader, I found that having a true doors-open policy was also about being willing to have open, honest, and transparent dialogue about the school, our teachers, and students with parents and families. In his book *How to Say the Right Thing Every Time: Communicating Well With Students, Staff, Parents, and the Public*, Robert D. Ramsey (2008, as cited in Ruder, 2006) states:

> When school leaders communicate effectively, students learn, parents and community members understand and support what the school is doing, and the process of teaching and learning moves forward. But when educators fail to communicate fully, misinformation, misinterpretations, misunderstandings, and mixed messages can cause the system's wheels to spin or come off altogether.

Creating a culture that allows parents to have access and dialogue with the principal, within reason, and being approachable and communicative greatly enhanced our parent and family relationships at Minnieville Elementary.

Using Home Visits

It's important to foster an open-door policy in the school; it's equally as important to foster a doors-open policy with parents and families. Educators should be available when parents and families come through the school doors, but what about meeting parents and families at their doors? Many school districts have established successful home-visit programs. Home visitations by teachers let parents and students know how much teachers care. Also, programs that provide time and funding for teachers to visit students and parents on their own turf are a way for teachers to learn more about their students, get the parents more involved in their child's education, and bridge cultural gaps that might occur between student and teacher. Most teachers report their home visits have a lasting effect on the child, the parent, and parent-teacher communication (National Education Association, n.d.).

The idea of home visits can be daunting to staff members. As an administrator, I have always been comfortable making home visits, but not all staff are so comfortable. To ease staff into the concept of conducting regular home visits, Minnieville Elementary's family-engagement guiding coalition organizes a summer "Books and Pops" event where staff members, PTO parents, and administrators visit each of the school's neighborhoods to give out free books and popsicles. We use social media to invite the community to meet the staff. Parents meet with teachers, and the staff become familiar with the neighborhoods, building positive relationships before the school year starts. The school's Books and Pops event also has a strong focus on learning, especially reading.

Home visits should never be held at random or without prior notice. Staff and administrators should make prior arrangements and ask for permission before going to a parent's home, just as they should also never visit a parent or family's home alone. Use home visits to meet with parents and families if they cannot attend a conference or meeting at the school. Home visits are a good way to check in on families that may need assistance. Educators can set up times with them to drop off supplies, food, or other resources. Minnieville Elementary staff have found that being accessible and supportive to families has greatly enhanced relationships and trust, creating stronger school-home partnerships.

The San Francisco Unified School District (n.d.) has created an excellent guide for home visits that could serve as a powerful resource for schools that includes sections on staff participation, staff preparation, a protocol and timeline for the visit, suggestions, and safety tips. It includes the following guidance. Staff should remember to:

- Be a good listener

- Have specific goals or objectives for each visit

- Be flexible

- Be prompt

- Realize the limitations of your role

- Help parents become more independent

- Keep language appropriate

- Dress appropriately and comfortably

- Be confident

- Remember that small improvements lead to big ones

- Be yourself

- Respect cultural and ethnic values

- Monitor your own behavior; the parent is observing you

PARENT *voices*

As the father of a fourth grader at Minnieville Elementary School, I would rate the school's customer service a 10 on a scale from 1 to 10. Minnieville has great communication, collaboration, outreach, and culture. I am always at ease whenever my daughter leaves the house to go to school. I know she's safe. I know if there's a question or concern that may arise, I can go to the school and speak with someone who is capable of addressing my question or concern. Minnieville has a very wholesome learning environment. At Minnieville, it begins with the first people you see as you walk in the secured front entrance, which adds another level of safety for parents worried about school safety. The first people you see are the warm, welcoming, nonjudgmental front office staff who never seem too busy to concentrate on your issue or need. They always make you feel like your concern or question is their priority. The administration and faculty at Minnieville definitely care about our children's best interests—not only with instruction, but also with being socially responsible, productive individuals. The administration and faculty are professional, transparent, and responsible. They undoubtedly listen to parents' concerns, feedback, and suggestions.
—Tracy Lamar Blake, Minnieville Elementary parent (personal communication, 2019)

Final Thoughts

Pay close attention to your school staff's efforts toward customer service. Does your school have a specific plan and structure for customer service and engagement? Or, is this an area that can be enhanced? Your school organization is a business with the sole purpose to ensure all students learn. Be mindful that the business of providing exemplary school customer service is the business of the entire school. The primary role of a school leader is to be an instructional leader. However, instructional leaders also must ensure the staff are implementing positive customer-service initiatives. Ensuring the building is inviting and safe to students, teachers, and families is vital. Ensuring the school's stakeholders have the resources they need to do their jobs as students, teachers, and parents is paramount. Ensuring all staff treat school stakeholders with kindness and respect regardless of the situation is a non-negotiable. In strong PLC cultures, there is a palpable environment of respect for all students, families, and staff. Staff treat every person who walks through the school doors like a valued contributor to the school's mission and vision. When school leaders are strategic about both customer service and customer experiences, the result will be an environment where students, parents, families, and teachers yearn to be!

Next Steps

In looking to create or improve your school's customer-service environment, the school's administration, along with teachers, parents, and family-engagement guiding coalition members, should consider the questions in the reproducible "Next Steps Tool for Chapter 4" (page 58).

Next Steps Tool for Chapter 4

1. What qualitative and quantitative data do we have access to that can inform us of our staff's customer-service efforts?

2. What areas could we improve in our school building to create a positive, welcoming, and lasting first impression for families, students, teachers, and visitors?

3. What specific customer-service training have we provided for our front office staff and teachers? What additional training may they need?

4. In examining the various events and opportunities for parents and families we host at our school, which events do parents, families, and community members best receive?

5. Is the current school and district policy for school visitors congruent with exemplary customer-service expectations? If not, how can we improve?

CHAPTER 5

CREATING A FOCUS ON LEARNING WITH FAMILIES

*To parents: We can't tell our kids to do
well in school and then fail to support them when they get
home. You can't just contract out parenting.
For our kids to excel, we have to accept our responsibility
to help them learn. That means putting away the Xbox
and putting our kids to bed at a reasonable hour. It means
attending those parent-teacher conferences and reading to
our children and helping them with their homework.*

—*Barack Obama*

According to DuFour et al. (2016), a focus on learning is the first big idea of a PLC; the fundamental purpose of a school should be to ensure all students learn at high levels. This focus on and commitment to the learning of each student are the very essence of a PLC.

Giving students every opportunity to learn and grow academically, socially, and emotionally is a school staff's primary focus. If students are not learning and growing each day, then the school staff are not doing their jobs. In a PLC culture, however, adult learning is just as important as student learning. In fact, if the adults in a school are not continually growing, learning, and expanding their professional practices, then student learning can't grow and expand. In a strong PLC culture, professional educators are not only seeking professional learning opportunities from their school, district, state, universities, and associations, they are also constantly enhancing their learning by engaging in collective inquiry and action research with every unit, lesson, and student.

Collaborative teams in PLCs utilize the four critical questions (DuFour et al., 2016) to determine (1) what students must learn (know and be able to do), (2) how teams will know when students have learned it, (3) how teams will respond when students haven't learned it, and (4) how teams will extend and enrich learning for students who have learned it. Teams gain a better understanding of standards; create, refine, and align their assessments; and use data for reteaching and enrichment.

In a strong PLC culture, everyone inside the building—adults and students—is growing as learners (DuFour et al., 2016). How, then, do strong PLC cultures grow the learning of the school community outside the school walls? What responsibility does the school staff have to focus on the learning of parents and families? I argue that strong PLC cultures have a tremendous responsibility for this. The question is, How can this be done effectively? Let's look at a hypothetical scenario that may help bring the answer to this question into focus.

Imagine a young family is enrolling their child for kindergarten at your school. This is the family's only child; the parents are nervous that their five-year-old will be spending eight hours of the day at a school away from the comforts of home. The family has looked at the school's website and Facebook page as well. As the parents enter the school, they meet the school secretary who answers questions and provides information about the enrollment process. One of the school's kindergarten teachers comes to meet them and is available to give the parents and student a brief tour of the school and answer questions. The teacher takes the parents and student into a kindergarten classroom and shows them the learning stations, morning meeting location, technology stations, and classroom library.

The teacher then shows the parents an area in the classroom with all the monthly learning targets clearly posted and outlined for the school year. This *learning target wall* has objectives and standards posted for the first quarter, and the teacher uses this board to explain to the family the expectations for kindergarten students at the start of the year and where they should be by the end of the first quarter. The teacher then gives the parents a folder that contains the same information. All the kindergarten standards are printed and in the folder, along with the expectations for the student for each month and quarter.

Next, the teacher hands the parents a plastic bag containing various resources their child may need at home to help him or her grow as a kindergarten student. In the bag are a few primary-level picture books, a small notebook, and crayons and markers for drawing pictures and practicing letter and word writing. In addition, the bag contains flashcards of letters, numbers, colors, and words for the family to use for practice with their child. The parents thank the teacher for taking the time to show them around the school and classroom and for explaining to them what the learning expectations are for their child. They also appreciate the resources the school provided to help them work with their child at home.

Now, let's consider a second scenario. Imagine a young family is enrolling their child for kindergarten at your school. Once again, this is the family's only child; the parents are nervous that their five-year-old will be spending eight hours of the day at a school away from the comforts of home. The family has looked at the school's website and Facebook page as well. As the family enters the office, they meet the school's secretary, who stops them to ask if they have an appointment. The family says *no*, but they would like to enroll their child in kindergarten. The secretary gives the family the enrollment paperwork and tells them if they have any questions about the school, they can look up the answers online.

Clearly, these two scenarios are vastly different. In the first scenario, the family enters a customer-friendly school environment where the staff and teacher have obviously taken the time to both build a relationship with the family and create a focus on learning. In the second scenario, the secretary's focus was on enrolling the child; he or she missed the opportunity to build a relationship with the family and create a focus on learning. Think about your school and what happens when staff enroll a student. Which scenario would most likely resemble your school? It's very possible that both schools in the scenario have strong PLC cultures in place, yet only the former sees the value of purposefully sharing the staff's focus on learning with the family.

This chapter examines how you can demystify learning (by answering the four critical questions of a PLC for parents and families), keep the focus on learning at school events, and focus on families as learners.

Demystifying Learning

School staff with a strong focus on learning do everything they can to demystify the learning standards, objectives, and targets for parents and families. Virtually all state education departments post their state curricula, standards, and objectives on websites that the public can access. The challenge for many schools is how to ensure that all parents and families have the opportunity to know how to interpret and understand their child's curriculum, objectives, and standards of learning. Parents and families should have access to the state learning objectives in multiple formats including digital access and hard copies. Provide parents with access to copies of state curricula and grade-level curriculum pacing guides at the start of the year. Show them how to access these plans and objectives via the school website. In addition, school staff should consider hosting quarterly grade-level information update nights, which parents can attend to learn about upcoming units of study. During these events, parents learn about strategies and teaching methods teachers will use in class and obtain various resources and materials they could use at home to help their child learn.

Furthermore, the teachers make parents aware of the standards for success for their child. Teachers could send this information to parents using email or messaging apps monthly or quarterly. It is important for schools to remember that just because parents and families have access to the curriculum standards, they may still need updates as to what their child is currently learning, how they will be learning, and how they will be assessed. At Minnieville Elementary, systematically and proactively sharing what students will be learning and how students will be learning it can greatly enhance both student performance and teacher instructional delivery. When parents and families are able to access and understand what their child will be learning, they can better support their child and their child's teacher.

Leveraging the Four Critical Questions

In high-performing PLCs, collaborative teacher teams constantly utilize the four critical questions throughout the year. If parents and families are partners in a school's collaborative efforts, then systematically teaching parents and families how to leverage the four critical questions as they advocate for their children's learning could be a game changer in a school's efforts to increase parent and family involvement and engagement and thus learning for all students. "The involvement of parents in the education of their children is of unquestionable significance. Students consistently indicate that student achievement increases as parents become more involved in their children's education" (Whitaker & Fiore, 2016, p. 11). Let's examine how parents and families can leverage each critical question to help their child learn.

Question One: What Is My Child Learning?

Parents and families are often uninformed about what their children are currently learning or will be learning in upcoming units. In Minnieville Elementary's efforts to ensure all students learn at high levels, all staff must be strategic about informing parents and families about what their children will be learning *before* the teaching happens; that way, they can prepare and play a role in ensuring their children's success.

In a PLC, collaborative teams carefully align their state standards with their yearly instructional pacing guides, creating instructional calendars and syllabi that lay out exactly what educators will teach, when they will teach it, and when they will assess it.

In a PLC focusing on building parent and family involvement and engagement, however, it makes sense for each teacher to provide parents and families with these documents at the start of the school year. Provide paper copies, online documents, or both!

Parents and families who have access to instructional pacing guides and calendars can strategically work to assist their children with the units of study; they have access to information that answers the often-unanswered question, "What did you learn in school today?" When a child replies, "I don't know" or "Nothing," the parent can pull out the instructional pacing guide, go to the date, and ask specific questions about their child's learning. If a parent didn't have access to the instructional pacing guide, the conversation might go like this, "What did you learn in school today?" The child replies, "I don't know." The parent then says, "Well, that makes two of us."

Pacing guides can be very overwhelming documents for parents and families and even for educators. One strategy teachers can implement to help parents and families work to understand the pacing guides, curriculum strategies, and objectives is to hold monthly or quarterly information nights to inform parents and families about what their children will be learning. At Minnieville Elementary, the third-, fourth-, and fifth-grade teacher teams, in collaboration with the school's mathematics specialist, host quarterly mathematics family information nights. These events allow family members the opportunity to meet with their child's teacher and learn about specific mathematics strategies and curriculum their child will be learning. These events have been extremely successful because they assist families in understanding the mathematics learning expectations. The way a parent might have learned a specific mathematics concept or strategy is often quite different than the way students are currently learning it.

Mathematics family information nights involve the mathematics specialist and grade-level teachers. The school provides food, childcare, and translation services during the event to assist families. At mathematics family information night, parents learn about the mathematics standards and objectives and practice the types of mathematics strategies their child will learn. They also learn how they can help their child at home with these math standards. After a brief overview on the mathematics standards and objectives students will be exposed to (separated by grade level), parents are then placed into smaller groups with their child to work on mathematics activities that focus on what students will learn. Parents receive copies of the curriculum and pacing guides, links to various online resources to help support their child's learning, and access to resources and materials that they can use at home with their child. These events allow both the families and teachers to be on the same page about curricula, teaching methods, and learning strategies.

In collaboration with the school's family-engagement guiding coalition, utilize the following three prompts to help parents and families feel confident in answering the first critical question, "What is it we want our students to know and be able to do?" (DuFour et al., 2016).

1. At the start of the year, our teachers provide parents copies and online access to the yearly pacing guides and instructional calendars.

2. Our teachers utilize technology to continuously communicate to parents what their child is learning and strategies they can use to help their child learn at home.

3. Our teachers create quarterly or monthly learning information nights for parents to teach them the strategies, resources, and materials teachers will use in the classroom.

Question Two: How Will I Know if My Child Has Learned It?

The second critical question of a PLC focuses on assessment and results. Traditionally, teachers inform parents and families of students' results by sending home graded work and report cards. Although helpful, informing parents of their child's results *after* the unit doesn't assist the student in mastering the standards. This practice, however, is typical in American schools and has been that way for decades. Imagine how powerful it would be if a teacher carefully articulates to parents how he or she will assess their children *before* the students ever take the assessment—if a parent and student have full knowledge that, at the end of the week, the teacher will assess the student on a ten-question multiple-choice quiz with a goal of passing at 80 percent (eight of ten questions). Imagine if the teacher communicates this via a weekly parent newsletter or using an internet-based communication software or apps such as ClassDojo, Remind, SchoolCNXT, TalkingPoints, and Bloomz (Common Sense Education, n.d.). If a parent has access to tools (such as a writing assessment rubric), the parent and student can have a more focused conversation about the expectations for writing with the teacher, and reinforce and support the school-home connection.

The importance of student grades is an area many parents and families resonate with. Whether a school or district implements traditional numerical or letter grading scales or incorporates standards-based grading within their practice, clearly informing and educating parents and families as to specifically how their child will be assessed on a particular activity, project, or assessment are important (Guskey, 2014).

To enhance the understanding and purpose of learning for each parent and family, schools should work to systematically inform parents and families of their child's progress in the classroom and what strategies, assessments, and expectations teachers will use to ensure each student is meeting standards and mastering the curriculum. To help parents and families with the second critical question, teachers should take the following three steps.

1. Provide parents with testing and assessment schedules and calendars both at the start of the year and each quarter.

2. Clearly communicate grading policies to parents and families.

3. Clearly communicate how you will grade various projects by sharing rubrics.

Question Three: What Will Happen if My Child Has Not Learned It?

To address the third critical question, collaborative teams in PLCs provide interventions for students who haven't yet reached proficiency. When schools implement intervention-based services, teams identify students in need of instructional services in addition to classroom instruction. In many schools, formal processes and programs are in place for students who need *strategic-learning plans* (that is, intervention plans, 504 plans, or individualized education plans [IEPs]). For the most part, parents and families are part of that formal process in schools. What happens, however, if a student simply needs more time on a particular task or a different strategy, modality of learning, or accommodation? Do your classroom teachers create a dialogue with parents and families to discuss what happens if their child does not learn the material the first time the educator teaches it? Parents and families should know what specific actions and modifications teachers will take to ensure their child has the chance to become proficient. Parents and families also should know how they can assist their child at home in learning the objectives. This level of involvement and engagement with parents and families can prove truly beneficial in helping students to become more proficient with standards and meeting their goals as learners.

PLCs that proactively inform parents and families about how staff respond when and if their child does not meet a standard show that learning is the school's primary focus. Teachers can share what specific strategies parents and families can implement at home to assist a child in his or her efforts to master the curriculum. These strategies could be in the form of various websites and learning software to help students with basic academic skills, additional reading materials, or even strategic practice opportunities with clear guidance on success criteria. When a teacher sends a graded assignment home, he or she can also provide the student and parents with clear feedback on what is necessary for the student to show proficiency and adequate progress on the task. This is vital for allowing the student and family to develop a clear understanding of what the student needs to do to master the curriculum. Teams and classroom teachers that systematically incorporate this level of instructional customer service greatly enhance the chance for all students to learn at high levels.

For a moment, consider a scenario where a parent requests a meeting with a school's principal. In that meeting, the parent asks the following questions.

- "How does this school track and monitor students in need of intervention?"
- "Currently, what percentage of students in the school receives special education services?"
- "What researched-based programs and services do you offer students in need of remediation?"
- "Are staff members who work with students in need of remediation highly trained and certified?"
- "Are students who receive intervention services pulled out of general education classrooms?"

As a school principal, teacher, or district administrator, are you prepared to answer each of these questions confidently? If not, you should be!

To help parents answer the third critical question, family-engagement guiding coalitions should consider the following three questions.

1. Do teachers and school intervention teams clearly communicate to parents the school's intervention system and framework?
2. Do teachers and intervention teams provide parents and families with ongoing access to remediation strategies and resources?
3. Do teachers provide students and parents with clear standards-based feedback on all assessments, projects, and assignments to help the student master the objective?

Question Four: How Will My Child's Learning Be Enriched and Extended?

The final critical question of a PLC typically answers how teachers will expose students who are already proficient with the objectives, standards, and curricula to experiences that enrich and extend their learning. Let's face it, some students seem to be born knowing much of a curriculum without ever setting foot in a classroom. Classroom teachers face the significant challenge of meeting the demands of learners with a wide variety of skills and background knowledge.

In his blog post, "Enrichment vs. Extension in the Regular Classroom," gifted intervention specialist for Lima (Ohio) City Schools Jeffrey Shoemaker (2014) states there is a difference between extension and enrichment. Shoemaker (2014) states *enrichment* projects are based on a topic the student is interested in and will lead to new in-depth learning on the standard the teacher is currently teaching. He says an *extension* activity extends or goes beyond learning the standard (Shoemaker, 2014). Many schools provide robust and extensive gifted-and-talented education programs for students, and these programs absolutely have a place in schools. However, there's often a misconception that it's just the gifted students who need enrichment or extension; but in PLCs, collaborative teams determine who requires extension and enrichment based on each specific learning target.

Collaborative teams of classroom teachers must strategically plan how to enrich and extend the learning for students who are academically proficient. In strong PLCs, teacher teams collaboratively plan for extension and enrichment of lessons for students *before* any teacher ever teaches the unit. Parents and families should know what specific strategies, materials, and resources their proficient child will have access to. Students will also benefit if teachers share the resources, materials, and strategies the families can use at home to help enrich and extend learning. Great teachers and teams know students' strengths and talents as learners; they have developed academic structures that allow students to take learning to higher levels.

As a classroom teacher, I recall working with some of the most gifted-and-talented students, who were often also extremely artistic, athletic, and creative. My task as a classroom teacher was to tap into their strengths and talents to help them integrate these assets into the curriculum. Provide parents with websites, materials, and resources they can use at home to enrich and extend the content.

Following is a list of websites and organizations parents and families could access to support the enrichment and extension of their child's learning (Open Education Database, n.d.).

- **Exquisite Minds (https://exquisite-minds.com):** Includes resources, online games, tips, tools, and more

- **The Gifted Child Society (www.gifted.org):** Nonprofit organization dedicated to furthering the cause of gifted children; includes offering helpful information as well as seminars and workshops

- **Hoagies' Gifted Education Page (https://hoagiesgifted.org):** Offers a bit of everything, from conference listings to tips on understanding a gifted child

- **Mensa for Kids (https://mensaforkids.org):** Offers monthly themes to get students reading and learning at an advanced level

- **National Association for Gifted Children (http://nagc.org/resources -publications/resources-parents):** Provides a wide array of resources and materials for gifted learners

- **Supporting Emotional Needs of the Gifted (SENG; https://sen gifted.org):** Helps ensure families, schools, and workplaces understand, accept, nurture, and support gifted children

- **TeachFine on Gifted Ed Tech (https://educationaladvancement .org/grc/teachfine-on-gifted-ed-tech):** A collection of resources that combine gifted education and technology

- **TeacherVision (www.teachervision.com/extension-enrichment -activities):** Cross-curricular extension and enrichment activities for teachers, supervisors, and parents

In assisting to help parents and families with the fourth critical question, consider the following three steps.

1. The teacher clearly communicates to parents and families how their child, who has achieved curriculum objectives, will have his or her learning extended and enriched.

2. The teacher provides parents and families access to materials, resources, strategies, and information on how they can enrich and extend their child's learning at home.

3. The teacher provides resources and materials to and seeks advocacy groups for parents and families that support gifted-and-talented learners.

Putting the Four Critical Questions Together

As this chapter shows, the four critical questions can be just as powerful for parents as they are for teachers in the school. To explore this concept further, consider the following parent-teacher conference scenarios.

At Freeman Elementary, parents and families arrive at the school and enter their children's classrooms for scheduled parent-teacher conferences. Teachers have reserved twenty-minute time slots to meet with each student's family members; teachers are prepared to share information such as how each student is currently performing, his or her grades, reading level, behavior, and so on. As Mia's parents enter the room, the teacher meets them and begins showing them Mia's work samples and grades. They chat briefly about her academic progress and behavior. But because of the time constraint, very little dialogue happens between the parents and the teacher, and the parents leave with a little more familiarity about how Mia is performing in the class.

Now let's imagine a different scenario that allows both the parents and the teachers to utilize the four critical questions as a road map for the parent-teacher conferences.

At Wilson Elementary, parents attend a back-to-school night at the beginning of the year and learn about the four critical questions. They learn how to use these questions effectively to understand their child's progress during a parent-teacher conference. As parents enter the school during the parent-teacher conference evening, administrators greet parents at the door and hand out a half sheet of paper reminding them to ask the four critical questions (What is my child learning? How will I know if my child has learned it? What will happen if my child has not learned it? How will my child's learning be enriched and extended?). Parents are well-prepared as they enter their child's classroom for their scheduled parent-teacher conference. The teachers have reserved twenty-minute time slots to meet with parents.

As Mason's parents enter the classroom, his teacher begins to share very specifically what standards he has worked on recently and will be working on in upcoming units. The teacher shares the assessments Mason completed, how he performed on those assessments, and the strategies she utilized when Mason didn't meet a standard. The teacher informs Mason's parents about resources they could use at home to help further support his learning a standard. For the standards Mason did master, the teacher explains what he did in school to enrich his learning and what resources and activities they could use at home to enrich and extend his learning. During the conference, both Mason's parents and his teacher have a clear understanding of the standards, how Mason is meeting the standards, how the teacher will assess Mason, how he is performing, and the desired outcomes. Finally, the teacher presents a clear explanation of the resources and strategies she is utilizing to help Mason grow as a learner.

In both scenarios, parents are an important part of the parent-teacher conference; however, in the second scenario, there is a clear, systematic *focus on learning*. There is also a concerted effort to utilize the four critical questions as a covenant between the school and home to ensure a focus on learning.

Focusing on Learning at School Events

In the seminal book, *Beyond the Bake Sale* (Henderson et al., 2007), the authors describe the levels of achievement in school-home partnerships. The highest level of achievement is a *partnership school*. In this type of school, "All families and communities have something great to offer—we do whatever it takes to work closely together to make sure every single student succeeds" (p. 15). Partnership schools ensure a link to learning with every event. Most school staff do an amazing job at building community by hosting after-school events like open houses, fall festivals, bingo nights, movie nights, father-daughter dances, spring flings, and so on. Although these events are important and fun for parents and community members, they don't always focus on learning. Partnership schools use events to focus on learning, highlight standards, give parents opportunities to reteach skills at home, and provide families with resources to help their children succeed.

At Minnieville Elementary, the planning committee incorporates a focus on learning at our yearly fall festival. Historically, the fall festival is our biggest school fundraising event; both parents and students have a wonderful time. The planning committee noticed, however, a lack of actual learning at the event and some missed opportunities for assisting families. With that knowledge, the planning committee makes sure each game focuses on skills such as sight words, number recognition, or even multiplication skills. Games like Guess the Weight of the Pumpkin reinforce measurement and estimation skills. Free books as prizes (instead of candy and plastic toys) focus attention on literacy. The library remains open during the event to help inform parents of new online resources they can use to help their children learn at home. Even with these changes, parents and students still have a remarkably fun time and, more important, gain a renewed focus on learning. School events that promote parent and family involvement absolutely have a role in schools. Simple adjustments to these events ensure student learning is still taking place.

Focusing on Families as Learners

So often in schools, the focus on learning pertains only to students. In strong PLC cultures, however, there is a focus on learning for students, staff, and families. Leaders of strong PLC cultures see the value in having every teacher and staff member actively learning and growing their professional practice to achieve better results for the students they serve (DuFour et al., 2016). Now, let's envision a culture where a focus on learning centers on students' families as well. Imagine a school that utilizes its resources to empower parents and families with strategies, materials, and programs that help them become better parents and advocates for their children. Staff in successful school cultures place a priority on this type of parent learning and actively work to seek resources, programs, and materials to help parents learn more about parenting, assisting their children with school work at home, advocating for their children, and partnering with their children's school.

For example, there are several programs developed specifically to assist families with parenting and advocacy skills for their child and school. A major tenet in the work of the U.S. Department of Education (USDE) focuses on this very topic. In 2010, the USDE Office of Communications and Outreach published *Parent Power: Build the Bridge to Success*. In this work, readers get practical ideas, strategies, and resources about how to be more involved and engaged parents (USDE, 2010). This booklet focuses on the following eleven simple ideas to help parents and families be better informed about their child's educational experience (USDE, 2010):

Be responsible.

Accept your role as the parent and make education a priority in your home.

Be committed.

Once you have begun to work with your child, continue doing so throughout the year.

Be positive.

Praise goes a long way with children, especially with those who struggle in school. Provide positive feedback.

Be patient.

Show your child that you care through your commitment and encouragement.

Be attentive.

Stop your child immediately when bad behavior appears. Show him or her what to do and provide an opportunity to do it correctly. Discipline should be appropriate and consistent.

Be precise.

Provide clear and direct instructions.

Be mindful of mistakes.

Record your child's performance. Look over all the work your child brings home from school and keep it in a folder. Help him or her correct any errors.

Be results-oriented.

Gather information on how your child is performing in school. Keep notes of conferences with teachers, request progress reports, and carefully read report cards and achievement test results. Ask questions about these results.

Be diligent.

Work from the beginning to the end of the year with your child and the teacher.

Be innovative.

Keep learning lively and dynamic.

BE THERE.

Just be there for your child—to answer questions, to listen, to give advice, to encourage, and to speak positively about his or her life. Be there to support your child whenever needed. (pp. 6–8)

PARENT *voices*

Before my daughter started her kindergarten year at Minnieville Elementary, she was openly nervous about going to school. Her fears of new surroundings, new expectations, and being out of her comfort zone were difficult for her to overcome. From our family's first experiences entering the school, however, we were met with the friendly faces of the front office staff, secretaries, custodians, and of course the amazing teachers. My wife and I spoke openly about what we hoped for our daughter, which was, "Is our daughter going to love her teacher, and is her teacher going to love her back?" This is a powerful question that speaks to the heart of what every school has to offer. After the first week of school, we asked our daughter what she thought about her new experiences in kindergarten; her response was telling. She said, "Daddy, I can't wait to go to school!" To any parent, that is the most important thing your child can say because it speaks to the positive and supportive culture built within the school and cultivated by the teachers in every classroom.
—Jonathan Alsheimer, Minnieville Elementary parent (personal communication, 2020)

Final Thoughts

In schools operating as PLCs, a focus on learning is center and paramount to every aspect of the school day. Strong PLC cultures focus on the learning of every school stakeholder. School staff strategically teach parents the four critical questions to utilize from a parent perspective. Teachers in strong PLC cultures take every opportunity to empower parents and families with curriculum documents and pacing guides throughout the year. School staff strategically host information nights to teach families about upcoming academic units of study, what their children will be learning, and how they will be learning it. They focus on learning both during and after school hours, creating events that build both community and academics. Teachers in strong PLC cultures help parents learn how to assist their children with learning at home. Staff utilize resources, materials, and programs to assist parents and families with how to be the best parent advocates for their child and their school. Parents are indeed their children's first teachers. As school cultures center on learning for all, let's make sure we as educators are giving parents and families every opportunity to learn along with us.

Next Steps

School administrative teams, along with your family-engagement guiding coalition, should consider the questions in the reproducible "Next Steps Tool for Chapter 5."

Next Steps Tool for Chapter 5

1. Do teachers explicitly teach parents the four critical questions? If not, how can we do this?

2. Do teachers give parents and families access to standards, curricula, and pacing guides throughout the year? If not, how can we do this?

3. Do teachers and teams strategically work with parents to teach them how to interpret curriculum and pacing guides? If not, how can we do this?

4. Have teachers clearly communicated to parents and families how district grading policies work? If not, how can we do this?

5. Have teachers clearly communicated how they will assess students using rubrics on project-based assignments? If not, how can we do this?

6. Have teachers clearly communicated the school's intervention processes to parents and families? If not, how can we do this?

7. Have teachers clearly communicated how students' learning will be enriched and enhanced when they master the units of study and objectives? If not, how can we do this?

8. Do our after-school events and programs have a focus on learning? If not, how can we improve?

9. Do our staff provide opportunities to enhance parent and family learning to assist parents in becoming stronger advocates for their children's learning? If not, how can we improve?

10. Based on the responses to these questions, what are some potential next steps and actions our school can take to enhance a focus on learning for parents and families?

CHAPTER 6

CULTIVATING COLLABORATION WITH FAMILIES

A single arrow can be broken,
but not ten in a bundle.

—Japanese proverb

School staff implementing the PLC process find that success cannot happen in a vacuum. In high-performing PLCs, all school staff remove barriers to collaborative practices among teams, teachers, and administrators. They implement systematic processes for collaboration. Teams collaboratively create norms that guide members' behavior during collaborative work. They systematically focus on the four critical questions of a PLC, carefully analyzing standards, and collaboratively creating assessments. Teams share ideas, strategies, resources, and best practices to improve each member's professional practice. They carefully analyze and disaggregate student data and create intervention and enrichment plans for each student. Collaborative teams in PLCs co-construct strategic goals to guide their efforts and hold one another mutually accountable for their success as professional educators. In strong PLC cultures, resource and specialty teachers find time to actively collaborate as well to ensure consistency in instructional efforts. In addition to grade- or course-level collaborative teams, guiding coalitions help teachers focus on carefully improving professional practice in reading, mathematics, student behavior, and other areas. PLCs truly understand that collaboration among teachers and teams is vital for success.

What roles can parents and families have in collaborating with schools operating as PLCs? This book presented many of these roles in previous chapters. This chapter discusses collaboration with formal parent organizations; families of second-language learners, middle-class families, and economically disadvantaged families; and the business community.

Collaborating With Formal Parent Organizations

Formal school-home partnerships such as with PTOs or PTAs (parent-teacher associations) are commonplace for most schools. These organizations are outstanding for their efforts to both increase family engagement and involvement in schools as well as to promote fundraising efforts. In schools that generally have higher numbers of involved parents and families, these associations and organizations play a huge role. In schools that have higher numbers of economically disadvantaged, culturally diverse, and immigrant families, parent participation in these organizations may be a challenge. Jen Cosgrove (n.d.), in her blog *School Volunteers Share*, notes that many parents don't volunteer for a formal parent-teacher organization for a variety of reasons.

1. **They are scared:** Some parents fear that if they agree to volunteer for an event or job, they will get "sucked into a 'black hole' of never-ending . . . requests for help" (Cosgrove, n.d.). Parents might worry that if they have only a small amount of time to give that it wouldn't be enough to make an impact. Parents might be scared of the stress and burnout that can come with taking on additional responsibilities. Parents might also be hesitant to volunteer for something that is beyond their comfort zone. They might feel intimidated by parent volunteers who have more experience.

2. **They can't fit volunteer opportunities into their schedules:** Some parents are able to help both at school or outside of school. However, more parents aren't able to help during school than are able because of work schedules. Schools will have difficulty filling parent volunteer slots if the available volunteer opportunities don't offer a variety of times and days or aren't flexible in nature to suit various parent schedules.

3. **The expectations are too high:** There are limits to how much time families are willing and able to give. If they feel that the PTO or PTA is too inflexible and wants too much from them, they might be unwilling to give any time.

The National Parent Teacher Association (n.d.) provides ten ways to get parents and families more involved and enthusiastic about volunteering.

1. **Explain the options:** Don't assume people know how to get involved with the PTA.

2. **Start small:** Help parents build strong relationships with one another, which usually leads to greater participation with broader school activities.

3. **Keep it personal:** Get to know parents. This makes it much easier to ask them for help.

4. **Say "yes":** Agree to any idea if a parent is willing to take the lead on it.

5. **Make it easy:** Create an inclusive online community. Set up chats about school and events. Put up requests for volunteers. Create an email newsletter.

6. **Ask for input:** Ask parents for their ideas and suggestions to fuel interest and motivation.

7. **Use visuals:** People notice images and talk about things that make them laugh. Use that to your advantage to get people involved.

8. **Share feedback:** Let parents know the benefits students and teachers receive from their efforts.

9. **Encourage nominations:** Ask parents to suggest other parents who have specific skills.

10. **Show your appreciation:** Thank parents for their help to show your appreciation. Parents will be more likely to continue participating if they feel valued.

The roles these formal parent organizations and associations perform can vary greatly from school to school. One of the goals of this chapter is to encourage school leaders to think about how to strategically increase collaborative efforts between their PLC and these organizations. In addition to these types of organizations and associations, many schools have parent-staff advisory councils. These councils generally include various school stakeholders, such as teachers, assistants, specialists, and administrators, as well as parents and family members. Parent-staff advisory councils assist administrators with tasks like budgetary overviews and school-improvement plan creation and review. During parent-staff advisory council meetings, members ask administrators questions about various issues and concerns regarding the school community. Both types of parent-school organizations significantly impact a school's focus on collaboration in positive ways. However, having formal parent-teacher organizations, associations, and advisory councils does not necessarily mean there is collaboration between parents and school staff.

So, what specific strategies can PLC leaders implement to increase collaboration with parents, families, and staff in these formal organizations? If schools have a formal PTO, PTA, parent-teacher-counselor organization (PTCO), or parent-staff advisory council, school leaders should pay close attention to the types of items and topics members discuss at meetings. Carefully evaluate agenda items and discussion topics to determine whether they align with the essential elements of PLCs. The principal and other school leaders should consider the following questions.

1. Do the topics of discussion at our parent meetings promote the mission and vision of the school?

2. Do the topics of discussion at our parent meetings promote student learning and school improvement?

3. Do the topics of discussion at our parent meetings allow for the discussion and review of instructional results?

4. Do our parent meetings utilize collaboratively created norms to help guide the work of members?

5. Do a wide variety of school stakeholders collaboratively create the agenda items for parent meetings?

6. Do parent teams understand how to reach consensus when making decisions?

7. Do the efforts of our parent-staff advisory council meetings promote and foster an increase in learning for parents and families?

8. Do the parent teams' fundraising efforts promote student and staff learning and foster growth of parent involvement and engagement?

9. Do the parent participants represent a diverse cross section of our school community?

10. Does the parent team construct clear goals to guide its work?

These questions can help school leaders better align their efforts with the PLC process elements. It is also vital for school administrators and leadership teams to ensure when parents come to school meetings to participate in the instructional process through a collaborative framework, they take parents' opinions, suggestions, questions, and concerns seriously into account.

Supporting and Communicating and Collaborating With Families of Second-Language Learners

One major demographic at Minnieville Elementary the staff and I were highly motivated in collaborating with was the non–English speaking parents and families. The Minnieville Elementary staff and I found our non–English–speaking parent and family population extremely diverse, coming from a wide array of socioeconomic backgrounds, ethnicities, and cultures. These parents often have different understandings and interpretations of the public-education process. Nonetheless, as with all parents, non–English speakers are crucial partners in supporting their child's success.

Lydia Breiseth (2011), manager of the educational outreach company Colorín Colorado, states in her work *A Guide for Engaging ELL Families: Twenty Strategies for School Leaders*:

> School leaders are in a unique position to create a culture of success within their school community. As with other students, an important aspect of ELL success is family engagement. While you may be fortunate to have an energetic and passionate ELL teacher or bilingual liaison who has worked successfully with ELL families in the past, this is not the job of a single person. Engaging ELL families can only work if *all* members of the community (including administrators, staff, parents, and students) are committed to the broader mission. The road will probably be bumpy at first and will most certainly require you to think outside of the box—the keys to your success may surprise you! In the end, though, the result is the same: parents, students, and educators working together towards a brighter future.
>
> When you find what works for your ELL families (which may or may not be the same as what works for the ELL families at a neighboring school), you will feel as though you have won the lottery. Engaged ELL parents possess depths of dedication and wisdom regarding their children that will take your breath away. They have so much to offer—if the community is ready to embrace them and listen to what they have to say. This is where you, as a school leader, can make important strides in changing the conversation from "What can they learn from us?" to "What can we learn from each other?" . . .
>
> Think of your ELL parents as a team waiting to be mobilized; while it will take some time and energy to get the team up and running (and to help them understand how valuable their contributions are), once everything is working, you will wonder how you ever got along without them! (p. 3)

Communicating with family members who do not speak English as their first language was a huge challenge for the staff at Minnieville. Actively working to consistently communicate the various aspects of schooling in English can be challenging enough, let alone doing so in multiple languages.

If you are unsure about what translation options are available, contact your second language educators or administrators from your school or district to find out more.

Note that some English-language or bilingual educators may be able to assist with translation, but they will likely have numerous other responsibilities, including communicating with students, planning their own instruction, and collaborating with other teachers, so they won't have a lot of time to dedicate. Options may include the following (Breiseth, 2020).

- **School or district interpreters, family liaisons, or paraprofessionals:** If your school or district has bilingual staff available to help with interpretation, ask your colleagues—

  - If and when they are able to assist with family communication

  - What process they prefer for setting up conversations

  - What worked or didn't work previously

  - If there are other translation resources that you should be familiar with

  - If families have common questions that can be addressed more efficiently

  - If there are some ways to make technical support in families' home languages more efficient

  - If there is anything you can do to support their work

- **District translation hotline:** Does your school district offer a translation hotline? If so, can you use it to set up conversations with families? If the hotline's hours don't match your families' availability, talk with an administrator about whether other options may be available.

- **Translation apps:** Ideally, districts will have in-person interpreters available in families' home languages. However, there are tools that can help, including TalkingPoints (talkingpts.org), an app that translates messages between teachers and families in many different languages.

ADMINISTRATOR *voices*

It is important for school leaders to take the time to learn about the background and cultures of each family. Oftentimes, our school's English learner (EL) families have come to the United States in search of better opportunities for their families and have tremendous assets to provide to the school. When school leaders and teachers take the time to learn about the rich diversity of their EL families, greater trust will flourish, which will equate to more opportunities to collaborate.

When working with parent-teacher organizations and family-engagement teams, create opportunities that highlight and showcase the diversity of the school routinely throughout the year. Show the school values the EL families' native languages by funding resources to support literacy in various languages and communicating important information in the major languages represented in the school. In working to build strong collaborative cultures with all parents in the community, school leaders and teams should seek representatives from a wide array of parents to ensure all families and communities are represented in the collaborative process as well. Doing so may necessitate the need for additional translators for parents as well as parent groups that collaborate in their native language.

School leaders should also be mindful that many ELs come from cultures that hold teachers in high reverence; in these cultures, teachers—not parents—are the experts. As a result, parents may be reluctant to ask questions so as not to question the teacher or principal's authority. As Betty J. Alford and Mary Catherine Niño (2011) note in *Leading Academic Achievement for English Language Learners: A Guide for Principals*, you wouldn't expect a doctor to ask the parents which medical procedure they would recommend for their child. EL parents may feel the same way about what their school is asking them to do.

Family engagement has increased as a topic of conversation in many schools. However, how many leaders make this a priority when crafting their school-improvement plans? This was something I grappled with as a principal. Coming from a school where the majority of students spoke Spanish, I found myself making a lot of mistakes regarding family engagement at my new school. As an assistant principal, I had felt comfortable connecting with families who spoke Spanish (my primary language) and sharing stories of encouragement and ways our educational system could support them.

Once I became a principal of Mary Williams Elementary, however, things changed. The school is known for its diversity and students who speak multiple languages. Most students came from Asia and Africa, meaning that traditions and family involvement looked different in several ways. I struggled. We typically saw mothers or older siblings attend activities. Our PTO meetings were barely attended, and I did not know where to start. This was something we needed to understand and become aware of as we planned activities that would support students and their families. Two of our staff members were from Africa; and once we started asking questions, we learned about many mistakes we were making in trying to reach them.

One of the first things we did as a staff was to include our family-engagement goals and strategies in our school-improvement plan. I once received advice from a mentor that "what gets monitored, gets done" (DuFour et al., 2016, p. 35). If we wanted our families to be involved, having every activity and school event tie to the needs of our community was a must. We carefully looked at our goals and crafted a plan that supported both families and instruction. As we audited our events and their attendance, we noticed more and more families attended and provided positive feedback on their experience. In everything we did, we became intentional about the connection of the offering to what students needed to be successful.

continued ▶

Being part of a diverse community meant staff needed to go beyond the multicultural night. For years we had tried to host one night a year when students brought dishes from their (native) countries and dressed to showcase their countries' outfits. While it was a lovely event, attendance was low. The teachers who did the planning could not figure out what the problem was and often felt disappointed, thinking they had done something wrong. After getting some feedback from the community, we learned we needed to go beyond the multicultural night. As a result, we started celebrating cultures all year round, dressing the school walls with our students' cultures, showcasing writings from their recent trips, and opening our classrooms to a variety of celebrations that recognized where students came from. Taking this approach taught us the value of having things like this in place to let students and their families know they belong in our school no matter where they come from.

As a school that embraced the PLC process, we wanted to ensure parents had a voice. Teachers met weekly and shared ideas at what I called the *dinner table;* then we began thinking, "Why could we not have families join us at the dinner table as well?" This can be a challenge for families who are English learners, as they might not know that schools can also serve as a resource for them. During parent-teacher meetings, our staff made it a point to ask all families for suggestions and feedback no matter where they came from. Translations were available, and our teachers became intentional about empowering parents to share their voice. During one of the meetings, one family suggested the idea of having a flyer with all the activities our school was having during the year. She explained that this would help her plan ahead and take off the days in advance. As we discussed this, our teachers took this idea further and divided all the activities into three categories: informational activities (PTO meetings, Math and Reading Instruction Nights, Meet the Teacher, and so on), family engagement (field day, music events, art events, reading night, book fair, and so on), and family involvement (field trips, carnival, and so on).

It took some time, but the lessons we learned as a staff were so valuable. It became our focus to plan programs based on the needs and interests of our families. From the way we communicated with parents to the activities we provided at the school, what began as a once-a-year event became *a way of living* where all students and their families had access to resources and support. —L. Colón, Director of EL Programs and Services in Prince William County, Virginia (personal communication, October 22, 2019)

Collaborating With Middle-Class Families

Middle-class parents are generally active participants in their children's schools and vocal advocates for both their children and the institutions they attend (Posey-Maddox, Kimelberg, & Cucchiara, 2014). These families can have a tremendously positive impact in supporting a school's efforts. "Public institutions frequently are more responsive to constituencies possessed of the 'sheer political clout' that tends to come with middle-class status" (Noguera, 2003, p. 33). With their higher levels of cultural, material, and social capital, middle-class parents could secure badly needed resources and raise standards for students and educators alike (Kahlenberg, 2001).

Oftentimes, middle-class families bring to the school setting resources, ideas, and partnerships that support both instructional and social programs for students. Middle-class families may have more opportunities to volunteer and support their child's teacher during the school day as well. In addition, middle-class families may be keener to support school-based instructional plans, and serve on budgetary committees, advisory councils, and parent-teacher organizations. Studies have suggested that the higher parents' income and education, the more likely they are to be involved in school; conversely, lower levels of education and income are correlated with lower levels of parental involvement (Cucchiara & Horvat, 2009). Actively collaborating with middle-class families can be an extremely positive partnership for schools.

ADMINISTRATOR *voices* ——————————————

Family engagement is at the heart of success for any elementary school. That is well-known and understood by many; however, purposeful engagement and planning are often not completely thought out. Hosting an event is only the tip of the iceberg when it comes to true, purposeful, well-attended family-engagement activities. At Centreville Elementary School (CES), we are passionate about connecting with our families in order to promote student success. We work to create family-engagement activities that provide learning experiences, community-building opportunities, and family-bonding time for our students and staff and their families.

We host several wonderful events to promote community engagement at CES. The school year starts off with a *welcome walk* the Tuesday prior to the first day of school. This is our unique way of letting students know who their classroom teacher will be for the school year. Our entire staff meets to go into the community and knock on the students' doors to notify them of their class placement and welcome them back after the summer break. The welcome walk lets our community know we are committed to them inside and outside of the brick and mortar walls of the school building. Two weeks later, we collaborate with our PTA to host a welcome-back picnic. This picnic is our most attended evening event during the school year. These first two events engage a large majority of our community and set the stage for a successful school year.

As the school year progresses, we offer several other events focused on collaborating, building positive relationships, and engaging our community, staff, and students. "A community that eats and learns together, grows together" is the mindset we use to focus the planning sessions for our monthly events. Throughout the year, we host monthly family dinner and STEAM (science, technology, engineering, arts and mathematics) nights. For these evening events, the school provides the main course and the families that attend bring side dishes and desserts. We engage in mealtime conversations with the purpose

continued ▶

of making connections to strengthen our relationships. Prior to and after the meal, hands-on learning stations are accessible for families to conduct experiments, construct inventions, and learn about local educational opportunities.

We offer family field trips several times during the year as well. These free weekend trips expose families to local destinations that impact our school and environment. Funding for these trips came from securing grants from various state agencies and our community partners. For example, we might go to a local composting farm, stream, river, or solar energy plant. The school provides transportation, background knowledge through information sessions, and interpreters if needed. The families provide the energy and excitement. It is a win-win situation!

Family Fitness 4 a Cause was established to engage families in physical fitness, character education, and service learning. Through this program, families participate in fun weekly training sessions working up to fitness events (walks or runs) that support a cause (homelessness, lymphoma and leukemia research, and others). While training, families learn about the cause and ways they can support it through service learning. The overall theme of this program is *character education*, with a focus on helping others.

Family engagement is just as important during the summer as it is throughout the school year. In the summer, we go back to our mindset of "A community that eats and learns together, grows together." Once a week during the month of July, we offer family summer nights. On these summer nights, we have a good old-fashioned summer cookout! We cook juicy burgers, plump hotdogs, and fresh garden vegetables on the school grill, open the school library for families to check out books, and develop family-learning stations. It is a great way to connect with our community.

CES is very proud of our family-engagement events. However, we also believe we can improve. The focus moving forward is to increase our engagement so that it is a better representation of our diverse community. To accomplish this, we have established a community-engagement team consisting of school staff and community members. The engagement committee must consider how it can adapt the PLC pillars (mission, vision, values, and goals). To do this, we modified the four PLC critical questions.

1. What do we expect our community to do and attend?
2. What does success look like, and how will we know if we are successful?
3. How will we respond if they do not attend?
4. How will we continue to increase our attendance and progress?

We will achieve success through our commitment toward collaborating, building positive relationships, and engaging consistently with our stakeholders. Also, because we believe in our school chant, "CES is the best!" —J. Douds (personal communication, September 15, 2019)

Collaborating With Economically Disadvantaged Families

Vinson (2007, cited in McDonald, 2010) defines disadvantage as: "a range of difficulties that block life opportunities and which prevent people from participating fully in society" (p. 1). McDonald (2010) goes on to say:

> Low income is one characteristic of disadvantage; however, it is commonly argued that disadvantage is more far-reaching than economic poverty alone. A complex, multilayered understanding that incorporates social exclusion and relative deprivation is used in current literature to conceptualize disadvantage. This gives a voice to the experience of disadvantaged people that includes not only a lack of financial resources, but also a lack of access to key services and a restriction on social contacts and community participation (Saunders, 2008). Disadvantage has a negative impact on family functioning and child development (Brooks-Gunn & Duncan, 1997; Evans, 2019). The chronic stress associated with poverty, for example, can impact an adult's parenting capacity (Centre for Community Child Health, 2009). Children growing up in poverty are more likely to experience learning disabilities and developmental delay (Brooks-Gunn & Duncan, 1997).

Because Minnieville Elementary serves a demographic with more than 70 percent of families considered economically disadvantaged, the school receives federal funding (Title I) that supports our efforts to enhance our parent involvement and engagement. At Minnieville, we acknowledged there were many variables that kept families away from our school. At the beginning of the journey, we found many staff members had a pervasive belief that one of the main reasons our families living in poverty didn't collaborate with us was because they simply didn't care. We quickly found out, however, this was not the case. In fact, research shows less than 2 percent of parents living in poverty are truly apathetic toward their child's education. The other 98 percent find that social, financial, and cultural barriers prevent them from being truly engaged (Constantino, 2016). Our job as a school was to find those barriers and remove them so families would feel they were true collaborative partners in the school's mission and vision. One of the most important mindsets school staffs must embrace to increase their collaboration with economically disadvantaged families is that they truly value their children's education and want them to be highly successful as learners. The lack of resources, however, is a tremendous barrier for many families to actively collaborate with their schools. It is vital for schools with populations of economically disadvantaged families to do everything they can to embrace and value these families' assets, viewpoints, and perspectives.

Following are some tips, ideas, and strategies all school staff can utilize to assist collaboration with economically disadvantaged families.

- **Treat all families with dignity and respect:** This may sound simplistic, but it necessitates repeating; ensure all staff truly value all families regardless of their financial circumstances.

- **Strategically work to build, repair, and sustain relationships with families and communities:** Developing a relationship of trust between practitioners and individual families is critical to engagement. "The following personal qualities can help to build a trusting relationship with a family: a nonjudgmental attitude; a respectful attitude; an encouraging and empowering approach; warmth and empathy; and being authentic" (Coventory, 2009, as cited by McDonald, 2010). Relationships with communities are also important. Families may be more likely to attend a service if it is known within and recommended by key groups, agencies, or parents and families within the local community.

- **Don't assume all families understand the language of school:** Oftentimes well-meaning educators speak to families in *educationese* (or jargon educators use) and use acronyms that may leave families feeling demeaned and belittled. Take the time to effectively communicate the issues and plans of the school in terms that everyone can understand.

- **If possible, provide transportation and childcare:** Transportation can be one of the biggest barriers to having parents and families be active members in school-based events. Work to utilize school-based funds to provide transportation for parents or host school-based collaborative meetings outside school grounds. At Minnieville, working to coordinate ride shares with parents in the community is a positive approach to increasing attendance. Collaborative efforts with our division's transportation services provide school bus transportation to parents and families during after-school events.

  Often, working families cannot effectively collaborate with the school staff because of childcare needs. School leaders can work with teachers, volunteers, and agencies to create childcare options at the school for families. For parent-teacher conferences, consider allowing classified staff or instructional staff to provide childcare options for parents and families. Seek out volunteers from scouting organizations or local churches to assist with childcare, providing all volunteers have been appropriately vetted. Seek out businesses that provide enrichment opportunities for children. These businesses may provide free enrichment classes for students at evening school events. Some examples of these businesses may include sports clubs, martial arts academies, and science academies.

- **Provide translation and communication services:** When working to increase collaboration with all families, ensure effective translation and communication services are available. Communication between parents and teachers is critical to the learning process for students. When there is good communication, teachers can keep parents updated about student achievements, behavioral problems, health issues, and so on, and aware of opportunities available to students. Parent-teacher communication apps help teachers communicate with families, and many are free. Kayla Matthews (2018) presents the following list with both free apps and paid apps.

  Free Apps—

  - TalkingPoints: TalkingPoints is a communications app that breaks down language barriers. Teachers can input messages in English, and the app translates them into dozens of languages. Recipients who don't speak English can reply in their native languages.

  - Bloomz: This messaging app allows teachers to do tasks like sending updates and reminders. There's also a behavior-tracking function and ways for teachers to show examples of student work during the school day.

  - Remind: This app can translate messages into dozens of languages. It also goes further with the capability of sending PDFs, photos, and voice clips. Teachers can send messages to individuals or groups. A shortcoming of Remind is that it offers only one-way communication; parents cannot respond to messages.

  Paid Apps—

  - ParentSquare: This app is a secure way for parents and teachers to talk to each other about school. Teachers can share events or files and send private messages. Parents can select to have their details visible or hidden; this can help parents connect with others who also make their information visible.

  - Edvoice: This app offers real-time messaging and lets users send messages to an entire district or school or messages focused on a single class.

  - SchoolMessenger: This app facilitates direct communication, and it offers optional add-on features, such as notifying authorized parties that a child arrived at school safely. The app also stores various kinds of student information so it's easily accessible.

- **Actively recruit and retain diverse family volunteers in parent-teacher organizations:** When implementing any parent-teacher organization,

PTO boards should ensure equal family representation based on the school's community demographics. Parent leaders should work closely with the school principal to ensure all families are represented in this organization.

- **Create links between school and home:** Strengthening the family's ability to support their children's academic achievement and other forms of success in school is a priority in high-poverty schools. Michael Sadowski (2004) identifies six activities that a school might consider in establishing links between home and school: (1) implement dual-language classes for students, (2) implement programs for English language learning and offer GED and parenting classes, (3) incorporate home-school liaisons (with fluency in the home language), (4) implement preschool and early literacy programs, (5) offer early student assessments, and (6) plan and attend community and school activities and events.

Collaborating With the Business Community

Finally, effective schools understand they not only want to establish and maintain strong collaboration with parents and families but also with their business community. The Council for Corporate and School Partnerships (n.d.) states:

> A partnership can be defined as a mutually supportive relationship between a business and a school or school district in which the partners commit themselves to specific goals and activities intended to benefit students and schools. In most cases, partnering is a win-win situation for all involved parties. In addition to improving the education experience, the business partners frequently will realize benefits as well, such as enhanced goodwill and a stronger presence in the community.

Strong schools generate strong neighborhoods, strong neighborhoods create healthy communities, and healthy communities are good for business. School leaders should intensely work to create strong relationships with local businesses, places of worship, and community organizations. As a school leader, I find that taking the time to visit local businesses, introducing myself, and sharing information about our school are tremendously successful endeavors. During these brief visits, business owners and managers are more than happy to inquire about how they can help provide resources and support to the school. The visits often lead to partnerships, with businesses providing volunteers, donations of resources and materials, and funding for numerous school-based projects. Minnieville Elementary's business partnerships have been so successful, the school was recognized multiple times with our school division's Business Partnership of the Year award.

Deborah Ellis, principal of Minnieville Elementary and the school's former assistant principal, is instrumental in seeking and maintaining these collaborative school-business partnerships. Another important resource for business partnerships is staff and family connections. For example, one of Minnieville Elementary's first partners was a sorority sister and church member of Principal Ellis, Tabatha Turman. Tabatha was doing work in other area schools, so Principal Ellis asked Tabatha if she was willing to support Minnieville Elementary with funding for various student enrichment opportunities.

COMMUNITY PARTNER *voices*

We recognize that participating in the welfare of our communities is important. IFAS cares and does so by giving back to the communities in which we live and work, realizing our company has an impact on our communities. I simply refer to this as paying *earth rent*. —Tabatha Turman, Founder, CEO, and President, Integrated Finance and Accounting Solutions (IFAS; personal communication, 2017)

Two of Minnieville Elementary's community partners are through spouses of staff members or former staff members. Brandon Walker, the husband of a former staff member, is a former office manager of Potomac Pediatric Dentistry. At the beginning of the school year, when families are getting their children new school clothes, shoes, and supplies, the staff of Potomac Pediatric Dentistry make sure students start the school year ready to learn with beautiful smiles on their faces. Through this partnership, students can receive dental education and a dental screening at no cost.

COMMUNITY PARTNER *voices*

Potomac Pediatric Dentistry feels that no child should be without dental care. We strive to provide children in our local community with the knowledge and education on how to better take care of their teeth. We want to be available to help those in need and to find a way to work with them to provide comprehensive dental treatment. Potomac Pediatric Dentistry cares and does so by giving back to the community through a *free dental day* for local families in need, as well as many other activities. To staff at Potomac Pediatric Dentistry, there is no greater feeling than knowing a child and his or her family has been helped through our partnerships. —Brandon Walker, Former Office Manager, Potomac Pediatric Dentistry (personal communication, 2017)

Another staff-initiated partnership was with Officer Dennis Jensen, the husband of a former teacher. With his assistance, Minnieville Elementary began a Minnieville Athletic Club in which third-, fourth-, and fifth-grade students develop teamwork skills and form mentor relationships with Prince William County police officers.

COMMUNITY PARTNER *voices*

I am very happy to have been involved with working with the students at Minnieville Elementary School. The opportunity to work and play with elementary students in a positive environment is something that we don't often get to do. Seeing the kids so happy to interact with us gives me great hope for the future of the youth in our community. The officers who have volunteered for this program have all been impressed with the friendliness and willingness of the kids to interact with us and accept us into their groups. Most of the officers who volunteered had only scheduled one or two meetings with the group. After their first day, they all volunteered for additional dates, many of them coming in on days off! We have all enjoyed interacting with the kids at Minnieville Elementary and look forward to continuing to grow with them in the future! —Dennis Jensen, Former School Resource Officer, C. D. Hylton High School, Woodbridge, Virginia (personal communication, 2018)

ADMINISTRATOR *voices*

I grew up in a small community where everyone knew each other and collaboratively contributed to the success of the community's children. Although Minnieville isn't located in small-town America and today we often lead lives where we do not know all our neighbors, I do believe that everyone still has a desire to collaboratively contribute to the success of schools in their communities. At Minnieville, it is our desire to make our elementary school the heartbeat of our community. In order to do this, we carefully analyzed our school community's assets, noting businesses, places of worship, community resources, and so on, that surround the school and could be a benefit to our school community. After looking at the assets, the next step is to ask for support. At the time we started this strategy, then-principal Nathaniel Provencio took the time to visit the businesses in close proximity to the school. As members of the same community, we knew area businesses would want to support education. We asked for continued support as we taught students in our school how to become better citizens in our community. It is important to articulate that today's students will be the responsible, respected community members of tomorrow. The support businesses provide now will have major benefits in the future! —Deborah Ellis, Principal, Minnieville Elementary School, Prince William County, Virginia (personal communication, December 4, 2019)

Final Thoughts

All staff in effective PLC cultures understand that collaboration does not happen by chance. School leaders must strategically create opportunities for all staff to effectively work together to ensure the school's mission and vision become reality. If we as school leaders believe parents and families are active contributors to their child's success as learners, then we must also strategically create structures that allow all families opportunities to effectively collaborate with teachers, school leaders, and parent-teacher organizations. Staff in effective PLCs understand that a community of learners means the community of learners both inside and outside the school environment. Work to network with other local schools; school building leaders and staff tend to work in isolation, missing opportunities to collaborate and plan with neighboring schools to address increasing parent and family involvement and engagement.

This chapter discussed effectively collaborating with various subgroups and stakeholders, and school-based leaders' shared insights on how they worked to enhance collaboration with their school populations. As a school leader, take the time to evaluate who is "sitting at the table" when making major school-based decisions, strategies, and policies. Do those participants equally represent all stakeholders in your school's organization? Michael Enzi (BrainyQuote, n.d.), a notable American politician, once said, "If you're not at the table, you're on the menu!"

Next Steps

School leadership teams, along with the family-engagement guiding coalition, should consider the questions in the reproducible "Next Steps Tool for Chapter 6" (page 92).

Next Steps Tool for Chapter 6

1. Do we provide all parents and families opportunities to collaborate on school plans and initiatives? If not, how can we do this?

2. Do we actively recruit all parents and families to volunteer both in- and outside the school? If not, how can we do this?

3. Does our school maintain a formal parent-teacher organization and encourage all parents and families to participate? If not, how can we do this?

4. Does our school actively maintain formal business and community partnerships? If not, how can we improve?

5. Does our school create opportunities for families to collaborate with other families from surrounding schools about school- and social-based issues? If not, how can we do this?

6. Does our school utilize a system of multilingual resources to effectively communicate and collaborate with all families? If not, how can we do this effectively?

7. Based on the responses to these questions, what are some potential next steps and actions our team can do to enhance a focus on collaboration for our parents and families?

CHAPTER 7

FOCUSING ON RESULTS
WITH FAMILIES

Success is a science; if you have the
conditions, you get the result.

—Oscar Wilde

The third big idea of the PLC process is a focus on results. *Results* are the reality of your intentions. As a school leader, I knew for our school to grow, the staff and I had to create a renewed transparency on our outcomes. We had to consistently and systematically hold ourselves accountable by the results of our efforts. We had to be highly strategic on utilizing both qualitative and quantitative data to measure how effective our actions are in improving student learning. A focus on results underscores the importance of process. As former school administrator, teacher, and coach Mike Schmoker (1999) states, "Concentrating on results does not negate the importance of process. On the contrary, the two are interdependent: Results [the moment revealed] tell us which processes are most effective and *to what extent* and where processes need reexamining and adjusting" (p. 4).

According to DuFour et al. (2016), PLCs must gather evidence of current levels of student learning, develop strategies and ideas to build on students' strengths and address weaknesses in that learning, implement those strategies and ideas, analyze the impact of the changes to discover what was effective and what was not, and apply new knowledge to the next cycle of continuous improvement.

For schools, teams, teachers, students, and families, results are the school's *true north*—the orienting point that helps them stay on track—in leading the way to the school's vision and mission. For schools looking to ensure families are integral in the school's success, leaders must continuously share the results of these efforts with parents, families, and the greater community to foster trust, transparency, and accountability for all students to learn at high levels.

This chapter discusses the importance of embracing your current reality, fostering a culture of growth, and sharing results to improve results.

Embracing Your Current Reality

As a school principal, I remember numerous conversations with prospective home buyers inquiring about our elementary school. One particular conversation I recall was with a visiting family that asked to meet with me one summer day to inquire about a tour of the school. This was one of my favorite aspects of my job, so I gladly stopped everything I was doing to interact with this family. After introductions, I asked them how they heard about our school. They said they were moving to the area and were looking for affordable homes close to highly rated schools. They found our school using a link on a real estate website. Knowing full well about these dubious websites, I asked what score our school was given. They said, "Six out of ten."

I began the tour by showing them a bulletin board in one of our main hallways that carefully articulated all our academic goals as a school and end-of-year data that showed our current reality in all subject areas. I explained that the previous year, 85 percent of students passed the mathematics end-of-year state assessment and 87 percent of our students passed the language arts reading assessment. I also shared that our school goal was for 90 percent of all students to pass the end-of-year state assessment in both language arts and mathematics. Additionally, I shared that our school had received multiple awards for our academic and social programs and had award-winning, highly trained staff members. I would also inform these parents that over 75 percent of our students qualified for free lunch and over 70 percent of our students speak a language other than English.

Later, I took the parents to my office and opened the same website they had used to find our school. I showed them a school nearby that received a 9 out of 10. I explained that the particular school was made up of white middle-class families from high socioeconomic backgrounds, had little diversity, and enrolled virtually no second-language learners. I then showed the family that school's state assessment data and compared its results to ours. I pointed out that our school's data were significantly higher than the other school's.

By having this results-based conversation, it was important to let our *school results* speak for themselves in assisting this family in making a decision about where to purchase their home and send their child to school. The family ended up enrolling their child at our school.

I share this story to illustrate that *results matter*. Again, the third big idea that drives the work of PLCs is the need for a results orientation. Members of a PLC recognize that all of their efforts must ultimately be assessed on the basis of results rather than intentions (DuFour et al., 2016). More important, results matter *in context*. As a leader, it was always important for me to highlight our student academic progress, whether it was great, good, or growing. When families are searching for their children's schools, they may not have the luxury to visit a school and sit down with the principal to learn about the school culture. They may simply go to a real estate website or even your school website to learn about your school. What you post, what others post, and what is not posted about your school on the internet or on social media will become the reality for many parents. Others will share your school data whether you like it or not. You might as well own what you have, articulate where you want to be, and highlight the strategies you are implementing to get there.

Fostering a Culture of Growth

As a parent, and former teacher and principal, I know the challenge of feeling like students are being over tested. I personally know the struggle of feeling like every other day I am quizzing, quick checking, exit ticketing, running records, and summatively assessing students. There is no doubt the No Child Left Behind Act of 2001 may as well have been named *No Child Left Untested*, and the Every Student Succeeds Act (2015), the *Every Child Succeeds on a Test Act*. Trust me—I get it. In all professions, *results matter*. Ensuring students are learning the curriculum standards at high levels matters, just like customer-satisfaction results matter in the service industry and home sales matter in the real estate industry. One of the main challenges for education leaders is carefully creating and fostering a culture of growth as well as proficiency (Dweck, 2017). It's one thing to say to a parent that the school's fifth-grade team is an excellent team of teachers who care for their students. It's another thing to say that the school's fifth-grade team is an excellent group of teachers who care for their students *and* have high student-achievement results.

Educators in PLCs own their data and student-achievement results. They know their student-achievement data points show students are either great, good, or growing. Strong leaders own student-achievement data regardless of their school's demographics, community situations, teachers, and so on. Strong leaders look at their results with a *no shame, no blame* attitude. They use data to show their current reality. They have a relentless focus on student achievement throughout the school year. Effective leaders know it is a waste of time to have a mission, vision, and specific schoolwide learning goals without a laser-like focus on concurrent student-achievement data week by week, month by month, quarter by quarter, and year by year. Strong leaders who foster a culture of transparency and trust document and share data with their community and use their current reality to highlight areas to celebrate or improve. If you are in a school where the results are not where they need to be, and you are asked to explain those results to parents and families, be ready to own your current data picture. Point out the specific strategies and actions your teachers and teams are ready to implement to ensure all students will make progress. Remember, no excuses, no shame, no blame—only growth toward goals.

Sharing Results to Improve Results

As school leaders look to share their current school reality with parents, families, and community members, it is important to highlight multiple areas and the many ways the school is trying to grow in addition to end-of-year test scores. As a school leader, I knew our end-of-year test scores were really just manifestations of the hard work and efforts of the students, teachers, staff, parents, families, and community throughout the year. So, the staff and I made a conscious effort to clearly track and monitor multiple measures of student growth. In addition to tracking and monitoring end-of-year test scores, we focused on the following data areas.

- On-grade-level reading rates
- Quarterly writing-prompt assessments
- Second-language literacy growth assessments
- Language arts, mathematics, science, and social studies formative and summative assessments
- Student-attendance data
- Behavior-referrals data
- Parent and volunteer hours

As part of our effort to systematically track and monitor these specific academic and social-emotional data points, the staff and I understood how important it was to clearly articulate to parents and families how we measured these data, the context for the shared results, and goals for each data point. The staff and I consistently shared the progress our school made on these data points with families in monthly newsletters and parent-advisory meetings, and included potential specific strategies the school staff may need to implement to assist in raising scores. Teachers monitored and updated data graphs in each classroom to show students how they were meeting their goals as a class, as well as data graphs for each student to highlight progress in meeting his or her personal goals as a learner. In sustaining a culture of PLCs, it is important for our students to understand the concepts of goals, strategies, and results in order to have true ownership of their learning.

The more transparent we were as a staff in sharing our data-based current reality, the more understanding our parents and families were in our efforts to raise scores. The more we communicated our growth as a school, the more ownership for academic success we had, according to parents. Because families had a better understanding of the school's attendance goals, attendance began to improve. Parents and families who may not have traditionally supported their child completing homework began seeing how important homework could be to enhance their child's mastery of the standards. Volunteer hours began to soar because families knew of our school's zealous monitoring of these hours. After a few years of making all schoolwide data points a priority for our school, our results began to take care of themselves.

Sharing data with parents, families, and the community does not have to be a cumbersome undertaking. Figure 7.1 (page 98) shows a simple form school leaders may utilize for taking the first steps in systematically sharing schoolwide data with their community. The form highlights a school leader's efforts to share various strategic academic and social data with the community, as well as the school's current reality, by quarter.

Final Thoughts

In strong PLC cultures, all stakeholders are integral participants in the effort to achieve high academic achievement for all students. Think about how your school currently shares its results with families. Do you consistently provide them with updated data points, or do they have to rely on real estate websites to see your school's scores? Do your students own their goals and data, and do they consistently share those data with their families? Regardless of where your school currently is on its journey, own your data and current reality. Share results as well as strategies for improving those results as you move from good to great. For parents and families, transparency builds trust, trust builds relationships, relationships build involvement, involvement builds ownership, ownership builds engagement, and engagement builds results.

Next Steps

School leaders, along with your family-engagement guiding coalition, should consider the questions in the reproducible "Next Steps Tool for Chapter 7" (page 99).

EXAMPLE: Schoolwide Data—Parent and Family Quarterly Update

Year: 2020	Percent of Students Reading at Grade Level		Language Arts End-of-Unit Average, Grades 3–5		Mathematics End-of-Unit Average, Grades 3–5		Schoolwide Attendance Average		Family and Community Volunteer Hours	
	Our Goal:	Current Reality:	Our Goal:	Current Reality:	Our Goal:	Current Reality:	Our Goal:	Current Reality:	Our Goal:	Current Reality:
Quarter One	75%	52%	70%	60%	70%	75%	90%	95%	200	150
Quarter Two	75%	60%	70%	65%	75%	75%	90%	80%	400	500
Quarter Three	80%	75%	75%	70%	75%	80%	95%	95%	600	700
Quarter Four	80%	78%	75%	70%	80%	85%	95%	93%	800	900
End-of-Year Average	80%	66%	80%	66%	80%	78%	95%	90%	1,000	1,400

Figure 7.1: Data-sharing form for parents and families.

Visit go.SolutionTree.com/PLCbooks for a free reproducible version of this figure.

Next Steps Tool for Chapter 7

1. Do we provide parents and families with opportunities to know and understand the school's current reality based on academic and social data? If not, how can we improve?

2. Are our school's data currently posted on our school website? If not, how can we improve?

3. Do teachers and teams transparently track and monitor data in the classroom? If not, how can we improve?

4. Do our students track and monitor their own personal academic progress? If not, how can we implement this strategy?

5. As a school, do we systematically create opportunities to inform our parents and families about our assessment processes and procedures and the success criteria students need to show proficiency? If not, how can we do this?

6. Based on the responses to these questions, what are some potential next steps and actions our team can take to enhance a focus on collaboration for our parents and families?

EPILOGUE

My hope for this book is to provide school leaders, teachers, and organizations familiar with the elements of the PLC process a pragmatic resource to assist them in growing parent, family, and community involvement and engagement in their schools. For nine years, I was extremely blessed to have the opportunity to serve a school that was both growing its efforts to implement the frameworks and components of a PLC while also working to enhance parent, family, and community involvement and engagement. These efforts served Minnieville Elementary well, helping it become one of the most decorated Title I schools in Virginia.

In this book, I reviewed the foundational elements of PLCs and highlighted the importance of schools having a strong mission and vision, creating and articulating strategic learning goals, and aligning all practices with a focus on learning, collaboration, and results. I discussed the necessity of schools having a customer-centric focus that shows value and appreciation to every parent, family, and community member who walks into the school building. I stressed the importance of creating a strong guiding coalition to help staff with their efforts to enhance parent and family involvement and engagement. Leaders discovered specific strategies to help utilize the three big ideas of a PLC to enhance parent, family, and community involvement and engagement. Finally, in the appendix, I will highlight resources and materials you can utilize to assist staff on the journey.

School leaders who are working to sustain a PLC culture know this is an ongoing process of collective inquiry and action research in which educators collaboratively work to achieve better results for the students they serve (DuFour et al., 2016). Every aspect of this book hinges on that belief and incorporates the foundational PLC elements to grow a school's parent, family, and community involvement. Even with the ever-changing educational dynamics in the world, schools that have a strong PLC culture that values every member of the school community will continue to strive for excellence whether educational services are through virtual or traditional means. For schools to grow as thriving education cultures, they must have the support of parents, families, and community members. It may be possible for a school to raise academic achievement and not focus on supporting parents, families, and community members. It is impossible, however, to *sustain* academic achievement without supporting them.

On your journey, remember to view all parents, families, and community members as vital members of your PLC. See your parents both as learners and as contributors to your learning and the learning of their children. See them as integral and necessary collaborators in your school's efforts to carry out its mission and vision. I deeply believe there is no such thing as a failing or at-risk school. All schools can achieve high results for every student. If schools work to incorporate the elements and structures of PLCs and include all parents as vital members of those structures, then student achievement will rise. If your school can do this, your chances of excellence will be tremendous!

ADDITIONAL RESOURCES AND MATERIALS

This appendix features additional resources, materials, activities, templates, and links to help support your school staff as they work to enhance parent, family, and community engagement. Although this list is not exhaustive, these resources will prove practical in helping your staff analyze where the school is on its journey, and help them align resources, create goals and strategies, and monitor efforts along the way.

Websites and Links That Support Family Engagement

America's Promise Alliance (n.d.), an educational organization that works to bring together nonprofits to grow and enhance the lives of America's youth, created the following comprehensive list of additional programs dedicated to enhancing the learning experiences for parents and families.

- **Annie E. Casey Foundation** [www.aecf.org]
  Provides grants for programs that support the most vulnerable children and families in America

- **ACT** [https://act.org/content/act/en/about-act.html]
  Provides college-planning resources for parents and students

- **American Academy of Pediatrics** [https://healthychildren.org /English/Pages/default.aspx]
  Provides a parenting corner with an assortment of publications relating to child health and development from birth through high school

- **Association for Middle Level Education** [https://amle.org]
  Provides a series of publications for parents around their involvement in their child's life during middle school

- **ASPIRA** [www.aspira.org/book/aspira-parents-excellence-apex]
  Provides resources for Latino parents to assist them in learning about negotiating change and improving education in their communities

- **Attendance Works** [https://attendanceworks.org/take-action /community-and-agency-partners/parents-and-parent -organizations]
  Provides information, including pledge cards, factsheets, toolkits, webinars, and research to parents, schools, and school districts

- **Boys and Girls Clubs of America** [https://bgca.org]
  Provides a variety of parent-engagement resources related to developing youth by strengthening families

- **Casey Family Programs** [https://casey.org/resources]
  Provides a variety of resources to support foster parents, care-givers, and birth parents

- **Child Welfare League of America** [www.cwla.org]
  Provides multiple resources and tips for all parents on raising children and working within the community to increase the support for parents and parenting

- **Children's Aid** [https://childrensaidnyc.org/programs /family-community#family_supports]
  Provides programs, workshops, technical assistance, preventive services, home-based services, and legal assistance

- **College Board** [https://parents.collegeboard.org/?excmpid =VT-00015]
  Provides college-planning resources for parents and students

- **Community Matters** [https://community-matters.org]
  Provides parent education workshops and staff
  development seminars

- **Corporate Voices for Working Families** [www.cvworkingfamilies.org]
  Provides research, reports, advocacy, and workshops

- **Families in Schools** [www.familiesinschools.org]
  Provides curricula, trainings, advocacy, outreach, custom capacity building, and grant opportunities

- **Families and Schools Together** [https://familiesandschools.org]
  Provides parent-involvement programs and prevention and
  intervention programs for parents, educators, law enforcement
  agents, chief brand officers, health care workers, and community
  members; also provides various after-school programs to schools
  and families

- **Military Child Education Coalition** [https://militarychild.org]
  Provides programs, workshops, support systems, resources,
  products, outreach through engagement, advocacy, and partnerships to ensure that all military children have access to
  inclusive, quality educational experiences

- **Mocha Moms** [https://mochamoms.org/i4a/pages/index.cfm
  ?pageid=1]
  Provides resources to support mothers of color who have cho-
  sen to not work outside the home in order to devote more time
  to their families and communities

- **National Association for College Admission Counseling**
  [https://nacacnet.org]
  Provides a variety of preparation and planning resources
  designed to help parents whose children are entering or
  preparing for college

- **National Association of Elementary School Principals**
  [https://naesp.org]
  Provides a variety of informational bulletins in English and
  Spanish for parents of elementary and middle school children

- **National Association of Secondary School Principals**
  [www.nassp.org]
  Provides an assortment of resources for secondary school principals related to parent and family engagement and involvement

- **National Black Child Development Institute**
  [https://nbcdi.org]
  Provides parent engagement resources to African American parents to help them become educated, motivated, and inspired to excel in all aspects of their child's life

- **National Center for Learning Disabilities**
  [https://ncld.org]
  Provides programs, research, and advocacy focused on helping individuals with learning disabilities to succeed

- **National Center for School Engagement**
  [www.schoolengagement.org]
  Provides program evaluation and assessment, research, technical assistance, and trainings to school districts, law enforcement agencies, courts, and state and federal agencies

- **Center on School, Family and Community Partnerships at Johns Hopkins University** [http://web.jhu.edu/CSOS /about.html]
  Provides resources for schools and educators around family and community involvement to help increase student success in school

- **UnidosUS [formerly National Council of La Raza]**
  [https://unidosus.org]
  Provides support for Hispanic Americans by conducting research, policy analysis, and advocacy

- **National Dropout Prevention Center/Network** [www.dropout prevention.org]
  Provides parents with family engagement resources and strategies for dropout prevention

- **National Fatherhood Initiative** [www.fatherhood.org]
  Provides multiple resources for fathers who are involved or would like to become involved in their child's educational success

- **National Foster Parent Association** [https://nfpaonline.org]
  Provides a list of organizations and resources that support foster parents and families to ensure positive educational outcomes for youth in foster care

- **National [Parental Information and Resource Centers] PIRC Coordination Center** [www.sedl.org/pubs/sedl-letter/v20n02/pirc.html]
  Serves as a technical assistance resource for PIRC, providing numerous resources relating to parent training and parent involvement in a student's academic achievement

- **National PTA** [https://pta.org]
  Provides an assortment of resources for parents and teachers around family involvement in a child's success in school from the largest volunteer advocacy association in the country

- **New Frontier 21** [www.newfrontier21.com]
  Provides educators and entire school districts with trainings centered on closing the achievement gap

- **Office of Head Start, Administration for Children and Families** [https://acf.hhs.gov]
  Provides numerous resources to build strong family and community partnerships with Head Start programs

- **ParentChild+** [https://parentchildplus.org]
  Provides programs that focus on early childhood literacy, school readiness, and parenting

- **Parents as Teachers** [https://parentsasteachers.org]
  Provides support and information on parent engagement in a child's early life, specifically pregnancy through kindergarten

- **Parents for Public Schools** [https://parents4publicschools.org]
  Provides networking, trainings, and advocacy to strengthen public schools

- **Prichard Committee for Academic Excellence's Commonwealth Institute for Parent Leadership** [https://prichardcommittee.org]
  Provides resources for parents centered around parent leadership, engagement, and partnerships

- **Raising a Reader** [https://raisingareader.org]
  Provides programming focused on developing literacy skills and
  routines in children

- **Reach Out and Read** [https://reachoutandread.org]
  Provides a model for promoting early literacy and school
  readiness by partnering with medical providers

- **The Rural School and Community Trust** [www.ruraledu.org]
  Provides a variety of services, including trainings, technical
  assistance, mentoring, and research to increase the capacity of
  rural schools to provide high-quality public education

- **Scholarship America** [https://scholarshipamerica.org]
  Provides resources for parents to guide them and their children
  through major life transitions, advocate for their children in
  school, and navigate college admissions and financial aid

- **Search Institute** [https://search-institute.org]
  Provides tools and information to assist parents to be more
  deeply and effectively involved in their children's lives

- **United Way** [https://unitedway.org]
  Provides information to parents and community partners of the
  importance of active participation in the education of children
  birth through age twenty-one, and the role United Ways across
  the country play in supporting education

- **U.S. Department of Education Parental Information and
  Resource Centers (PIRC)** [www2.ed.gov/programs/pirc
  /index.html]
  Provides information about the Department of Education's
  support for Parental Information and Resource Centers (PIRCs)
  and resources for parents in supporting their children in all
  aspects of their education

- **Zero to Three** [www.zerotothree.org]
  Provides trainings and information on the development of
  infants and toddlers [information added] (America's Promise
  Alliance, n.d.)

Tools to Assess, Plan, and Reflect on Parent and Family Engagement in Your School

Use the following tools (see figures A.1–A.4, pages 110–113) to assess, plan, and reflect on parent, family, and community engagement in your school.

Figure A.1 (page 110) is a tool the school can utilize to assess where they are in their efforts to increase parent, family, and community engagement using the elements of PLCs.

Figure A.2 (page 111) is a scheduling template school teams can use to outline and align their school-based parent and family-involvement and engagement events.

Figure A.3 (page 112) is a data-reflection form school teams can utilize to communicate school-based assessment results to their families.

Figure A.4 (page 113) is a list of question starters school teams can utilize to assist members in analyzing their current reality in their efforts to increase parent and family engagement.

Directions: On a scale from 0–4 (0 = Preinitiating, 1 = Initiating, 2 = Implementing, 3 = Developing, 4 = Sustaining), analyze where your school currently is in its efforts to align its PLC practices with parent, family, and community engagement for each area. Add up your scores to see where your school is based on the rubric. Use the data to create next steps and actions for your school or team.

Focus on Learning	Focus on Collaboration	Focus on Results
1. _____ All families know and understand the mission and vision of the school.	9. _____ All families have opportunities to collaborate on school plans and initiatives.	18. _____ The school communicates all academic and social results to families throughout the year.
2. _____ All families receive the standards, objectives, and instructional pacing for their child at the beginning of the year.	10. _____ The school actively recruits parents and families to volunteer both in- and outside the school.	19. _____ The school shares individual student-learning outcomes with families throughout the year.
3. _____ The school strategically provides multiple opportunities for families to learn about the curriculum, instructional materials, and resources throughout the year.	11. _____ All families have opportunities to co-create goals and initiatives for their child.	20. _____ The school celebrates student-, class-, grade-level-, and school-performance data with families throughout the year.
4. _____ The school creates multiple opportunities, resources, and materials to assist families in improving their learning as caretakers.	12. _____ The school creates and maintains a formal parent-teacher organization and encourages all parents and families to attend.	21. _____ Parent-teacher conferences reflect collaborative conversations that focus on goals and results.
5. _____ All school-based events have a focus on objectives and curriculum standards.	13. _____ The school actively maintains formal business and community partnerships.	22. _____ The school strategically communicates with families about all school-, district-, and state-based assessment results and their impact on the school and student.
6. _____ The school creates multiple opportunities to integrate family backgrounds, heritage, and cultures into the curriculum.	14. _____ The school creates opportunities for families to collaborate with other families from surrounding schools on school social-based issues.	23. _____ The school places a high value on customer service and the customer experience for all families and utilizes surveys to acquire stakeholder feedback.
7. _____ All families understand the school's procedures to support intervention and enrichment.	15. _____ The school utilizes a system of multilingual resources to effectively communicate and collaborate with all families.	24. _____ The school strategically tracks and monitors parent and family volunteer hours.
8. _____ The school exposes all parents and families to the four critical questions of a PLC.	16. _____ The school actively utilizes social media platforms to create two-way communication with families about the school.	25. _____ The school clearly communicates student performance on classwork to families using standards-based grading techniques.
	17. _____ The school allows families access to school-based materials and resources.	
Subtotal: _____	Subtotal: _____	Subtotal: _____

26. 0–25 = Preinitiating; 26–50 = Initiating; 51–75 = Implementing; 76–85 = Developing; 86–100 = Sustaining

Figure A.1: PLC-based parent-, family-, and community-engagement rubric.

Visit go.SolutionTree.com/PLCbooks for a free reproducible version of this figure.

With your guiding coalition, use this template to plan your yearly school-based activities based on function.

Month	Fundraising	Student and Parent Learning	Parent and Family Involvement	Staff, Parent, and Family Engagement
August				
September				
October				
November				
December				
January				
February				
March				
April				
May				
June				

Figure A.2: School-event calendar template.

Visit go.SolutionTree.com/PLCbooks for a free reproducible version of this figure.

Family Data-Reflection Form

The following data sources show our school's goals and current reality. Please let us know if you have any questions or concerns regarding our school's current progress.

Year	Percent of Students Reading on Grade Level	Language Arts Assessment Data, Grade ___	Mathematics Assessment Data, Grade ___	Schoolwide Attendance Average	Family and Community Volunteer Hours
Quarter One Goal					
Quarter One Reality					
Quarter Two Goal					
Quarter Two Reality					
Quarter Three Goal					
Quarter Three Reality					
Quarter Four Goal					
Quarter Four Reality					
End-of-Year Goal					
End-of-Year Reality					

Figure A.3: Data-reflection form template for families.

Visit go.SolutionTree.com/PLCbooks for a free reproducible version of this figure.

Parent- and Family-Engagement Action Plan

Utilize the following questions to create an action plan to assist in increasing your school's parent and family engagement.

1. What is our current reality regarding parent and family involvement and engagement?

2. What are our potential obstacles in this area?

3. What data sources do we have to support this area?

4. What data sources will we need to measure and monitor success in this area?

5. For this school year, what should our SMART goal be in this area?

6. Who will be responsible for monitoring the results for this goal?

7. What specific resources and materials will we need to meet this goal?

8. What specific actions will we implement to meet this goal?

9. How will we know when we are successful in this area?

10. How will we celebrate our efforts when we meet this goal?

Figure A.4: Parent- and family-engagement action-plan questions.

*Visit **go.SolutionTree.com/PLCbooks** for a free reproducible version of this figure.*

REFERENCES AND RESOURCES

Adams, D. (1976, January). *Parent involvement: Parent development* [Research report]. (ERIC Document Reproduction Service No. ED186511)

Ahmed, A. (2019, March 14). *Importance of mission vision in organizational strategy.* Accessed at https://smallbusiness.chron.com/importance-mission-vision-organizational-strategy-16000.html on September 11, 2020.

Alford, B. J., & Niño, M. C. (2011). *Leading academic achievement for English language learners: A guide for principals.* Thousand Oaks, CA: Corwin Press.

America's Promise Alliance. (n.d.). *Organizations with expertise in parent engagement.* Accessed at https://americaspromise.org/organizations-expertise-parent-engagement on April 9, 2020.

Blankstein, A. M., & Noguera, P. (2016). *Excellence through equity: Five principles of courageous leadership to guide achievement for every student.* Alexandria, VA: Association for Supervision and Curriculum Development.

BrainyQuote. (n.d.). *Michael Enzi quotes.* Accessed at https://brainyquote.com/quotes/michael_enzi_501997 on April 9, 2020.

Breiseth, L. (2011, August). *A guide for engaging ELL families: Twenty strategies for school leaders.* Washington, DC: Colorín Colorado. Accessed at https://colorincolorado.org/guide/guide-engaging-ell-families-twenty-strategies-school-leaders on May 27, 2020.

Breiseth, L. (2020). *Communicating with ELL families during COVID-19: 10 strategies for schools.* Accessed at www.colorincolorado.org/article/covid-ells-families on September 11, 2020.

Brooks-Gunn, & Duncan. (1997). The effects of poverty on children. *The Future of Children, 7*(2), 55–71.

Buffum, A., Mattos, M., & Malone, J. (2018). *Taking action: A handbook for RTI at Work.* Bloomington, IN: Solution Tree Press.

Byrnes, M. A. (2012). *There is another way! Launch a Baldrige-based quality classroom* (2nd ed.). Milwaukee, WI: ASQ Quality Press.

Careaga, R. (1988). *Parent involvement: A resource for the education of limited English proficient students* (Program Information Guide Series No. 8). Washington, DC: National Clearinghouse for Bilingual Education. (ERIC Document Reproduction Service No. ED337036)

Casas, J. (2017). *Culturize: Every student. Every day. Whatever it takes.* San Diego, CA: Dave Burgess Consulting.

Centre for Community Child Health. (2006). *Quality in children's services* (Policy Brief No. 2). Melbourne: Centre for Community Child Health.

Chen, G. (2020). *Parental involvement is key to student success.* Accessed at www.publicschoolreview.com/blog/parental-involvement-is-key-to-student-success on October 30, 2020.

Classlist. (n.d.). *Want more volunteers? 10 easy ways to get parents involved with the PTA . . .* [Blog post]. Accessed at https://blog.classlist.com/pta-volunteers on September 11, 2020.

Cleave, P. (2017, March 10). *Customer satisfaction surveys—why they are important?* [Blog post]. Accessed at https://blog.smartsurvey.co.uk/why-are-customer-satisfaction-surveys-so-important on September 10, 2020.

Common Sense Education. (n.d.). *Best messaging apps and websites for students, teachers, and parents.* Accessed at www.commonsense.org/education/top-picks/best-messaging-apps-and-websites-for-students-teachers-and-parents on September 11, 2020.

Constantino, S. M. (2016). *Engage every family: Five simple principles.* Thousand Oaks, CA: Corwin Press.

Conzemius, A. E., & O'Neill, J. (2014). *The handbook for SMART school teams: Revitalizing best practices for collaboration* (2nd ed.). Bloomington, IN: Solution Tree Press.

Corporate Finance Institute. (2015). *Smart goal.* Accessed at https://corporatefinanceinstitute.com/resources/knowledge/other/smart-goal on September 10, 2020.

Cosgrove, J. (n.d.). *School Volunteers Share.* Accessed at www.schoolvolunteersshare.com on September 11, 2020.

Cotton, D. (2015). *Key management development models: 70+ tools for developing yourself and managing others.* Harlow, England: Pearson Education Unlimited.

The Council for Corporate and School Partnerships. (n.d.). *A how-to guide for school-business partnerships.* Accessed at www.nhscholars.org/School-Business%20How_to_Guide.pdf on September 14, 2020.

Cucchiara, M., & Horvat, E. (2009). Perils and promises: Middle-class parental involvement in urban schools. *American Educational Research Journal, 46*(4), 974–1004.

Doganieri, E., & van Munster, B. (Writers). (2001). *The amazing race* [Television series]. Santa Monica, CA: CBS Studios.

DuFour, R., & DuFour, R. (2012). *The school leader's guide to Professional Learning Communities at Work.* Bloomington, IN: Solution Tree Press.

DuFour, R., DuFour, R., Eaker, R., Many, T. W., & Mattos, M. (2016). *Learning by doing: A handbook for Professional Learning Communities at Work* (3rd ed.). Bloomington, IN: Solution Tree Press.

DuFour, R., & Eaker, R. (2009). *Professional Learning Communities at Work: Best practices for enhancing student achievement.* Moorabbin, Victoria, Australia: Hawker Brownlow Education.

Dweck, C. S. (2017). *Mindset.* London: Robinson.

Edwards, D., Prokity, S., & Stevens, H. (2016). *Building a high achieving school: 3 C's to success* (2nd ed.). Lynchburg, VA: Warwick House.

Evans, L. (2019, May 30). *Southwest Airlines Co.'s mission statement & vision statement (an analysis).* Accessed at http://panmore.com/southwest-airlines-vision-statement-mission-statement-analysis on September 10, 2020.

Every Student Succeeds Act of 2015, Pub. L. No. 114–95, 20 U.S.C. § 1177 (2015).

Ewing, P. E. (1982). *The ABCs of special education: A handbook for parents.* Washington, DC: U.S. Commission on Civil Rights.

Ferguson, E. (2019, February 13). *Walmart's mission statement & vision statement, generic & intensive strategies.* Accessed at http://panmore.com/walmart-vision-mission-statement-intensive-generic -strategies on September 10, 2020.

Ferlazzo, L. (2011). Involvement or engagement? *Educational Leadership, 68*(8), 10–14. Accessed at www.ascd.org/publications/educational-leadership/may11/vol68/num08/Involvement-or -Engagement%C2%A2.aspx on April 8, 2020.

Ferlazzo, L., & Hammond, L. A. (2009). *Building parent engagement in schools.* Columbus, OH: Linworth Books/Libraries Unlimited.

Galloway, M., Conner, J., & Pope, D. (2013). Nonacademic effects of homework in privileged, high-performing high schools. *Journal of Experimental Education, 81*(4), 490–510.

Glossary of Education Reform. (2013). *School culture.* Accessed at www.edglossary.org/school-culture on September 11, 2020.

Gunn, J. (2018, June 27). *Wow-factor schools: 8 ways to build an awesome school culture.* Accessed at https://7mindsets.com/wow-factor-schools-8-ways-build-awesome-school-culture on September 11, 2020.

Guskey, T. R. (2014). *On your mark: Challenging the conventions of grading and reporting.* Bloomington, IN: Solution Tree Press.

Henderson, A. T., Mapp, K. L., Johnson, V. R., & Davies, D. (2007). *Beyond the bake sale: The essential guide to family-school partnerships.* New York: New Press.

Honigsfeld, A., & Dove, M. G. (2015). *Collaboration and co-teaching for English learners: A leader's guide.* Thousand Oaks, CA: Corwin Press.

Hopkins, G. (2005). *Does your school's atmosphere shout "welcome"?* Accessed at www.education world.com/a_admin/admin/admin424.shtml on August 04, 2020.

Hubspot. (n.d.). *Sophia Bernazzani.* Accessed at https://blog.hubspot.com/service/author/sophia -bernazzani?hubs_signup-url=blog.hubspot.com%2Fservice%2Fcustomer-service-books&hubs _signup-cta=null on September 11, 2020.

Hyken, S. (2011). *The amazement revolution: Seven customer service strategies to create an amazing customer (and employee) experience.* Austin, TX: Greenleaf Book Group Press.

Kahlenberg, R. D. (2001). *All together now: Creating middle-class schools through public school choice.* Washington, DC: Brookings Institution Press.

Kansas Parent Information Center. (n.d.). *Family engagement surveys.* Accessed at www.education .ne.gov/wpcontent/uploads/2017/07/Family_Engagement_Surveys.pdf on September 10, 2020.

Kellen. (2018, December 20). *Six apps for parent-teacher communication.* Accessed at https://blog. tcea.org/six-apps-for-parent-teacher-communication on August 10, 2020.

Kofman, F., & Senge, P. (1995). Communities of commitment: The heart of learning organizations. In C. Sarita & J. Renesch (Eds.), *Learning organizations: Developing cultures for tomorrow's workplace* (pp. 15–43). Portland, OR: Productivity Press.

Kotter, J. P. (2012). *Leading change.* Boston: Harvard Business Review Press.

Kowalski, T. (2010). *Public relations in schools* (5th ed.). New York: Pearson.

Lambert, L. (2003). *Leadership capacity for lasting school improvement.* Alexandria, VA: Association for Supervision and Curriculum Development.

Mapp, K. L., Carver, I., & Lander, J. (2017). *Powerful partnerships: A teacher's guide to engaging families for student success.* New York: Scholastic.

Marzano, R. J., Waters, T., & McNulty, B. A. (2006). *School leadership that works: From research to results.* Heatherton, Victoria, Australia: Hawker Brownlow Education.

Matthews, K. (2018, December 20). *Six apps for parent-teacher communication.* Accessed at https:// blog.tcea.org/six-apps-for-parent-teacher-communication on August 10, 2020.

Mattos, M., DuFour, R., DuFour, R., Eaker, R., & Many, T. W. (2016). *Concise answers to frequently asked questions about Professional Learning Communities at Work.* Bloomington, IN: Solution Tree Press.

Meyer, P. (2019, February 20). *McDonald's mission statement & vision statement (an analysis).* Accessed at http://panmore.com/mcdonalds-vision-statement-mission-statement-analysis on September 10, 2020.

Moon, Y., & Quelch, J. A. (2003). *Starbucks: Delivering customer service.* Boston: Harvard Business School.

Morgan, B. (2018, March 5). *Customer experience vs. customer service vs. customer care* [Blog post]. Accessed at https://forbes.com/sites/blakemorgan/2018/03/05/customer-experience-vs-customer -service-vs-customer-care on April 8, 2020.

National Association for Family, School, and Community Engagement. (2010). *Family engagement defined.* Accessed at https://nafsce.org/page/definition on April 8, 2020.

National Coalition for Parent Involvement in Education. (2006). *Research review and resources.* Accessed at www.ncpie.org/WhatsHappening/researchJanuary2006.cfm on September 16, 2011.

National Education Association (n.d.). *Research spotlight on home visits.* Accessed at www.useaut .org/tools/16935.htm on October 30, 2020.

National PTA. (n.d.). *The Center for Family Engagement.* Accessed at https://pta.org/center-for -family-engagement on April 8, 2020.

Nike. (n.d.). *About Nike.* Accessed at https://about.nike.com on August 10, 2020.

No Child Left Behind Act of 2001, Pub. L. No. 107–110, 20 U.S.C. § 6319 (2002).

Noguera, P. (2003). *City schools and the American dream: Reclaiming the promise of public education.* New York: Teachers College Press.

Ohio Department of Education. (2009). *Conducting the the Parent and Family Involvement Survey for your school(s): Instructions and guidelines.* Accessed at https://in.gov/sboe/files/ODE-Family -Involvement-Instructions-and-Survey.pdf on May 28, 2020.

Open Education Database. (n.d.). *48 essential links for parents of gifted children.* Accessed at https://oedb.org/ilibrarian/50-essential-links-for-the-parents-of-gifted-children on April 9, 2020.

Palermo, J. (2017, August 30). Principal: Free school supplies level the playing field at Minnieville Elementary. *Prince William Times.* Accessed at www.princewilliamtimes.com/news/principal-free -school-supplies-level-the-playing-field-at-minnieville-elementary/article_e487bf3d-29a5-57c4 -bfe6-1cea46f01313.html on September 10, 2020.

Panorama Education. (n.d.). *User guide: Family-school relationships survey.* Accessed at https://panorama-www.s3.amazonaws.com/files/family-school-survey/User-Guide.pdf on April 8, 2020.

Pfeil, M. P. (1980). *Title I, ESEA: Working with schools—A parent's handbook.* Washington, DC: Division of Education for the Disadvantaged, Bureau of Elementary and Secondary Education, U.S. Office of Education.

Pink, D. H. (2018). *Drive: The surprising truth about what motivates us.* Edinburgh, Scotland: Canongate Books.

Posey-Maddox, L., Kimelberg, S. M., & Cucchiara, M. (2014). Middle-class parents and urban public schools: Current research and future directions. *Sociology Compass, 8*(4), 446–456.

Prince William County Public Schools. (2018). *Minnieville Elementary School: 2017–18 school profile.* Accessed at https://minnievillees.pwcs.edu/UserFiles/Servers/Server_408622/Image /Minnieville%20Elementary%20profile.pdf on April 8, 2020.

Project Appleseed. (n.d.). *Benefits & barriers to family involvement in education.* Accessed at www.projectappleseed.org/barriers on September 10, 2020.

Reglin, G. L. (1993). *At-risk "parent and family" school involvement: Strategies for low income families and African-American families of unmotivated and underachieving students.* Springfield, IL: Thomas.

Rowland, C. (2019, February 13). *Apple Inc., mission statement and vision statement (an analysis).* Accessed at http://panmore.com/apple-mission-statement-vision-statement on September 11, 2020.

Ruder, R. (2006). Approach & visibility. *Principal Leader, 7*(3), 39–41.

Sadowski, M. (Ed.). (2004). *Teaching immigrant and second-language students.* Cambridge, MA: Harvard University Press.

San Francisco Unified School District. (n.d.). *A guide to home visits.* Accessed at www.healthiersf.org /Forms/parentFamily/A%20Guide%20to%20Team%20Home%20Visits.pdf on September 11, 2020.

Sanborn, M. (2004). *The Fred factor: How passion in your work and life can turn the ordinary into the extraordinary.* New York: Currency.

Sasser, W. E., Jones, T. O., & Klein, N. (1999, March). *Ritz-Carlton: Using information systems to better serve the customer—Harvard Business School Case 395–064, October 1994.* Accessed at hbs.edu on October 26, 2020.

Saunders, P. (2008). Measuring wellbeing using non-monetary indicators: Deprivation and social exclusion. *Family Matters, 78,* 8–17.

Schmoker, M. (1999). *Results: The key to continuous school improvement* (2nd ed.). Alexandria, VA: Association for Supervision and Curriculum Development.

Schmoker, M. (2006). *Results now: How we can achieve unprecedented improvements in teaching and learning.* Alexandria, VA: Association for Supervision and Curriculum Development.

SchoolDigger. (n.d.). *Minnieville Elementary.* Accessed at www.schooldigger.com/go/VA/schools /0313001308/school.aspx?t=tbRankings on April 8, 2020.

Shoemaker, J. (2014, April 4). *Enrichment vs. extension in the regular classroom* [Blog post]. Accessed at https://ramblingsofagiftedteacher.wordpress.com/2014/04/04/enrichment-vs-extension-in-the -regular-classroom on April 8, 2020.

Sinek, S. (2009). *Start with why: How great leaders inspire everyone to take action.* New York: Penguin.

Solution Tree. (n.d.). *PLC at Work: The DuFour Award.* Accessed at https://solutiontree.com/awards /dufour-award on April 8, 2020.

Southwest. (n.d.). *About Southwest.* Accessed at https://southwest.com/html/about-southwest/index .html on April 8, 2020.

Spector, R., & McCarthy, P. D. (2000). *The Nordstrom way: The inside story of America's #1 customer service company* (2nd ed.). New York: Wiley.

Spector, R., & Reeves, B. O. (2017). *The Nordstrom way to customer experience excellence: Creating a values-driven service culture* (3rd ed.). Hoboken, NJ: Wiley.

Stuart, T. S., Heckman, S., Mattos, M., & Buffum, A. (2018). *Personalized learning in a PLC at Work: Student agency through the four critical questions.* Bloomington, IN: Solution Tree Press.

Tech Notes. (2019, January 7). *Six apps for parent-teacher communication* [Blog post]. Accessed at https://blog.tcea.org/six-apps-for-parent-teacher-communication on September 14, 2020.

Travers, J. (2018). *What is resource equity?* Accessed at www.erstrategies.org/cms/files/4039 -what-is-resource-equity-oct-2018.pdf on September 11, 2020.

U.S. Department of Education. (n.d.). *Family and community engagement: Engaged families build community.* Accessed at www.ed.gov/parent-and-family-engagement on May 27, 2020.

U.S. Department of Education. (2008). *Helping families by supporting and expanding school choice.* Accessed at www2.ed.gov/nclb/choice/schools/choicefacts.pdf on August 10, 2020.

U.S. Department of Education. (2010, June). *Parent power: Build the bridge to success.* Washington, DC: Author. Accessed at www2.ed.gov/parents/academic/help/parentpower/booklet.pdf on April 8, 2020.

Vinson, T. (2007). Dropping off the edge: The distribution of disadvantage in Australia. Melbourne: Jesuit Social Services.

Wallace Foundation. (2012, January). *The school principal as leader: Guiding schools to better teaching and learning.* New York: Author. Accessed at www.wallacefoundation.org/knowledge-center/ school-leadership/effective-principal-leadership/Documents/The-School-Principal-as-Leader- Guiding-Schools-to-Better-Teaching-and-Learning.pdf on January 7, 2012.

Whitaker, T., & Fiore, D.J. (2016). *Dealing with difficult parents* (2nd ed.). New York: Routledge.

White House Initiative on American Indian and Alaska Native Education. (2015). *The Every Student Succeeds Act.* Accessed at https://sites.ed.gov/whiaiane/nsei/the-every-student-succeeds-act-essa-2015 on September 14, 2020.

Williams, K. C., & Hierck, T. (2015). *Starting a movement: Building culture from the inside out in professional learning communities.* Bloomington, IN: Solution Tree Press.

INDEX

Learning by Doing, 3rd Edition
Richard DuFour, Rebecca DuFour, Robert Eaker,
Thomas W. Many, and Mike Mattos
Discover how to transform your school or district into a high-performing PLC. The third edition of this comprehensive action guide offers new strategies for addressing critical PLC topics, including hiring and retaining new staff, creating team-developed common formative assessments, and more.
BKF746

The Big Book of Tools for Collaborative Teams in a PLC at Work®
William M. Ferriter
Build your team's capacity to become agents of change. Organized around the four critical questions of PLC at Work this comprehensive resource provides an explicit structure for collaborative teams. Access tools and templates for navigating common challenges, developing collective teacher efficacy, and more.
BKF898

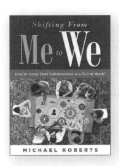

Shifting From Me to We
Michael Roberts
Rely on this straightforward guide to help you build the foundation of a true PLC. Packed with answers to common questions, *Shifting From Me to We* details how leaders at all levels can navigate frequent roadblocks to foster a strong, collaborative culture.
BKF946

AllThingsPLC Magazine
AllThingsPLC Magazine features engaging, personal commentaries from educators who have implemented the PLC process to great success. Each issue of this practical and stimulating quarterly magazine includes in-depth articles on PLC implementation and advice, websites, books, and other essential PLC resources.
CPF001

Solution Tree | Press

a division of
Solution Tree

Visit SolutionTree.com or call 800.733.6786 to order.

Wait! Your professional development journey doesn't have to end with the last pages of this book.

We realize improving student learning doesn't happen overnight. And your school or district shouldn't be left to puzzle out all the details of this process alone.

No matter where you are on the journey, we're committed to helping you get to the next stage.

Take advantage of everything from **custom workshops** to **keynote presentations** and **interactive web and video conferencing**. We can even help you develop an action plan tailored to fit your specific needs.

Let's get the conversation started.

Call 888.763.9045 today.

SolutionTree.com